Images of Jesus

ANSELM GRÜN

Images of Jesus

Translated by

JOHN BOWDEN

continuum
NEW YORK • LONDON
www.continuumbooks.com

The Continuum International Publishing Group Inc
370 Lexington Avenue, New York, NY 10017

The Continuum International Publishing Group Ltd
The Tower Building, 11 York Road, London SE1 7NX

Translated from the German *Bilder von Jesus*,
published by Vier-Türme GmbH Verlag,
Münsterschwarzach 2001

First published in English 2002

Library of Congress Cataloging-in-Publication Data

Grün, Anselm.
  [Bilder von Jesus. English]
  Images of Jesus / Anselm Grün ; translated by John Bowden.
    p. cm.
  ISBN 0-8264-6781-4 (hardcover)
  1. Jesus Christ—Person and offices. I. Title.
  BT203 .G7813 2002
  232—dc21
                                                    2002013241

Typeset by SetSystems Ltd, Saffron Walden, Essex
Printed and bound in the United States of America

Contents

Part III: Epilogue

Part I
Prologue

A new Jesus book for a new time

In my monastery, from time to time a small group talks about spiritual questions and what people are interested in today.

Recently we've been particularly preoccupied with the person of Jesus of Nazareth. We asked ourselves how far Jesus really shapes and changes our lives. Does Jesus influence our daily lives? Does he help us to cope with our everyday fears, conflicts and disappointments? What is really fascinating about Jesus of Nazareth? What is his message for us today in this world? These and similar questions kept cropping up. We felt that we owed ourselves and the people who come to our monastery as guests an answer to them.

The conversation also kept turning on how Jesus is seen outside our monastery. What role does he play in the life of men and women at the beginning of the new millennium? What images do they have of Jesus? Are these images attractive or repulsive? We realized how many clichés about Jesus there are. It's become almost impossible to get a good idea of his person, his life and his real significance.

We felt that it was time to write a new book about Jesus, a book that showed Jesus as he really was. It had to be a book that aroused interest in the rabbi from Nazareth, that made people curious to get to grips with Jesus again.

We didn't want to work out a systematic theology, but simply to offer a series of images that showed Jesus in a different light and opened our eyes to characteristics of this great man that we hadn't known before.

Images are forms of transport

Images don't stay still. They're like windows through which we look at a distant view. Each window offers us a new view. Images are an invitation to us to form yet other images of our own. Images open our eyes. But we're also free to pass over an image if it says nothing to us.

Images seek to open windows so that we see Jesus in a new way. Images show something of Jesus that a conceptual theology can't describe. Up-to-date images disclose new aspects of the figure of Jesus. Images are forms of transport. They get us going. They move us on. But sometimes our transport stops. It doesn't go any further. Then we have to change to another form of transport; we have to look for other images that allow us to discover new aspects of Jesus.

We looked for traditional images of Jesus and also some unfamiliar ones, which may perhaps seem uncongenial at first sight. We deliberately wanted some disturbing images which didn't reflect the usual ineffective clichés that keep cropping up in many sermons and homilies. The images here are meant to help us. They set out not only to show Jesus in a different light but also to invite us to a new art of living. The images of Jesus are always also images of a fruitful way of living.

However, we also have theological reasons for our decision simply to offer a series of images of Jesus instead of writing a systematic history or theology of Jesus. The images show us that in the end of the day we can't grasp Jesus, that he keeps evading all the terms we use of him. On the other hand, the images that we've chosen haven't been plucked out of thin air. They're all images that are meant to bring us close to the historical Jesus. Jesus is a historical event. His life and his influence can be reconstructed from the information in the Gospels. The Greek Luke put the events of the life of Jesus in a historical framework as early as AD 90. It was important for him that Jesus changed history. Jesus' history doesn't end with his death. It continues. A movement extends all over the world from Nazareth in Galilee via Jerusalem, the holy city of Judaism, until it finally reaches Rome, the capital of the Roman empire. This movement continues to the present day and has transformed history more than any other event.

7 BC to AD 30: Jesus of Nazareth, the historical event

Many scholars are studying the history of Jesus at the present time. They aren't content with just reading the theology of the communities which produced the Gospels. In particular, scholars living in Israel and every day experiencing life in its landscape are giving us new insights into the historical Jesus. Jesus was born in the year 7 (or 6) of our era. He grew up in Nazareth, a small village in Galilee with between 100 and 150 inhabitants. Probably in the year 28 he went to the Jordan valley, where John had been baptizing since around 26. From March 28 Jesus lived in Capernaum, where he started his public activity. John was arrested in November 28. Now Jesus really began his mission. In March 29 John was executed. Jesus was active above all in Galilee, but every year he went up to Jerusalem for the feast of the Passover. There he preached in the temple and expelled the merchants from the temple precinct. By doing this he provoked above all the Sadducees, who benefited financially from the trade in the temple. On 7 April 30 Jesus was crucified by the Romans and died on the eve of the Passover feast. His disciples fled back to Galilee. There Jesus kept appearing to them.

Spiritual currents in Israel in the year o

There were four different groups in Israel in the time of John the Baptist. The Sadducees formed the priestly nobility. They were devoted to the temple cult and denied the possibility of resurrection. They were probably Jesus' real enemies, the ones who handed him over to the Romans. If we were to look for today's Sadducees, we would find them in the influential business circles which are always concerned only to maintain their own power and to silence any political and religious trouble-makers.

The Pharisees were the largest group. They attempted to protect the laws that God had given to the people with a hedge of subsidiary laws. Jesus had many discussions with the Pharisees. He didn't reject them, but in his interpretation he was much more gentle and free than most of them. Presumably the polemic against the Pharisees which is evident in the woes that Jesus proclaims on them, above all in the Gospel of Matthew, should be largely attributed to the evangelist. After the destruction of Jerusalem by the Romans in 70, at the synod of Jamnia the Pharisees resolved to expel the Christians from the synagogue. Only from this period on did the Christian communities see the Pharisees as their real opponents. Jesus himself had very good relations with individual Pharisees. Basically the Pharisees were pious people who therefore made efforts to live in accordance with God's will. They had a hard time under Roman rule, but they tolerated it as the fate that God had given them. Nowadays we could imagine the Pharisees as circles interested in religion, concerned to maintain tradition and live a pious life in the midst of a secularized world. Jesus respected the Pharisees, but clearly dissociated himself from them when their interpretations were prompted too much by fear rather than by the will of God, who wants human beings to have a good life and not to be slaves under the burden of the law.

A third group was the Essenes. These were originally priests, but around the middle of the second century BC they had left the service of the temple and retreated into the wilderness. They thought that the temple cult was unclean and replaced ministry in the temple with ritual washings by which they hoped to cleanse themselves from their guilt. There were both married and unmarried Essenes. The Essenes had monastic-type centres in Qumran, on the south-west hill of Jerusalem (present-day Zion), and near Damascus. John the Baptist had been an Essene, but left the Essenes to engage in his own mission. A large number of the first Christians came from the Essene movement. Some scholars think that the last supper was held in an Essene guest house and that Pentecost took place in the Essene quarter. Jesus never engages in polemic against the Essenes. Only at a few points does he dissociate himself from them, as for example when in the parable of the unjust steward he says that the 'children of this world' are wiser in dealing with their like than the 'children of light'. The expression 'children of light' refers to the Essenes. They led a pious life in small groups. But anyone who violated the norms was rigorously expelled. Jesus doesn't want his disciples to exclude people but to welcome them into their houses (Luke 16.8).

The fourth group was the Zealots. They were the terrorists. Sometimes they are also called Sicarii, after the concealed daggers that they carried, with which they murdered so many Romans. The Zealots preached violent resistance against the Romans and also engaged in terrorist activities. Among the apostles Luke mentions Simon 'called the Zealot' (Luke 6.15). Presumably John and James, the two 'sons of thunder', also had a Zealot background. The surname of Judas, Iscariot, could mean that Judas was a 'Sicarius', a 'dagger man', in other words a Zealot terrorist. So Jesus had dealings with all four groups in the Judaism of the time. However, he didn't belong to any group, but went his own way.

A challenge: what you can do with these images

The fifty images of Jesus that we selected all relate to this man from Nazareth who lived from 7 BC to AD 30, who died on the cross, was buried and rose again. They seek to bring before our eyes the Jesus who lived 2000 years ago, so that we can understand him afresh for our lives and attempt to live in a different way. The images are an invitation to look with Jesus at our everyday conflicts, our problems at work and in the family, our anxieties and worries, our hopes and joys, and to deal with them differently. The images of Jesus are images of a fruitful life. They're meant to throw open the window behind which we so often hide. They're meant to broaden our lives, which so often have become too narrow, to make us do more than just sit around, constantly preoccupied with ourselves.

I don't expect you to read this book through at a sitting. I want to invite you to meditate on an image of Jesus every day or every week and to live with this image. Then you'll discover how this Jesus brings out new aspects of yourself and takes you into new areas of being human and encountering God.

You will be attracted by some images, but perhaps you won't know what to make of others. No one needs to take on board all the images of Jesus. The images invite you to look at Jesus from all sides and then examine your own life from his perspective. How can I live a good life in the sight of this figure, who doesn't leave me alone, who unsettles me and provokes me? At the end of each image I shall give you some suggestions about how you can understand the image as a challenge. Some questions are meant to invite you to reflect, and the exercises that I suggest should help you to shape your life by Jesus.

At the end I want to give an account of what Jesus means personally to me and how I live by my relationship with Jesus Christ. How far does Jesus stamp my personal prayer, thought and action? How do I deal with this Jesus of Nazareth in practice? How can I live by him? How do I experience healing, liberation, encouragement and life in encounters with him? How far is he 'my saviour'? Can I join Peter in saying, 'Lord, you know everything, you know that I love you' (John 21.17)?

Part II
Fifty Images of Jesus

I

Jesus the Jew

In the last thirty years many Jewish authors have rediscovered Jesus as a Jew. And Christian theologians, too, are beginning to make this discovery.

Jesus grew up as a Jew. He went to a Jewish school, learned to pray the psalms, and studied Jewish history as this is described in the Old Testament. He learned how to think and to live as a Jew. And as an adult he also took part in the discussions of the various Jewish schools. In his thinking Jesus remained Jewish. But his sovereignty became evident from the way in which he intervened in the discussion between the different trends within Judaism.

In his thinking, this Jesus from the little village of Nazareth shows a breadth that cannot be explained by any school education. He trusts his heart. He interprets the law as seems right to him in his innermost being. He is confident that he knows the will of God, not only for himself but also for others.

A German scholar, Wilhelm Bruner, who wrote a book called *How Jesus Learned to Believe,* has described how Jesus grew up in the Jewish tradition and learned his faith there. According to Bruner, his mother Mary was close to the apocalyptic tendency that was widespread in the Judaism of the time. That is evident from the Magnificat, her song of praise. Apocalyptic expected the imminent coming of God. And if God is coming, then the whole world will be turned upside down. The balance of power will be defined differently: the rich will be sent away empty and the hungry will eat their fill. Jesus learned from Mary that God would come soon to judge and to change this world. God has to be reckoned with. God will not delay but will go into action. God isn't a mere observer from outside. God intervenes in this world.

According to this same author, Joseph, who according to Matthew was a just man, belonged to the movement of the Pharisees, who set out to fulfil God's commandments. But Joseph wasn't zealous for the law. He associated righteousness, doing the right thing, with goodness and mercy. Had he simply been a just man, concerned only to fulfil the commandments, he would have had his pregnant wife accused on a charge that could have led to her death. However, Joseph didn't want to do justice to the law but to his fiancée. As he understood it, righteousness aimed at human well-being and wholeness. To do justice to the individual, one sometimes has to set oneself above the law as this has been written down and handed on. Jesus learned from Joseph to interpret God's laws in a merciful way.

In his religious education Jesus got to know the various spiritual schools in the Judaism of his time. Jewish scholars assign him to one of the more liberal Pharisaic schools. Jesus was influenced by the discussions then current in Jewish circles. He himself grappled with the law. He respected it, but he was also broad-minded enough to depart from it when it no longer did justice to actual men and women. Jesus was firmly convinced that the law was there for human beings, not vice versa. Everything that God commands us is aimed at helping us to live properly and to get on with one another, thus creating a sphere in which men and women can flourish together.

Jesus prayed the psalms. He took part in synagogue worship. And as a pious Jew, time and again he went on pilgrimage to Jerusalem, to join in the great festivals. There he experienced just how fascinating the temple and temple worship were. But although he grew up in this spirituality, Jesus developed a piety of his own. He had a very personal relationship with God. And because he had such an intimate relationship with his God that – unlike anyone else before him – he addressed God with the tender word 'Abba' ('dear Father'), he spoke of God in a new way. He was confident enough to talk about God differently, to draw a different image of God from the one that many of his contemporaries were used to. People had the impression that if someone spoke about God rightly, God really appeared in his words: 'And the people were astonished at his teaching; for he taught like someone who has (divine) authority, and not like the scribes' (Mark 1.22). Jesus didn't talk about God like many of the scribes, who used the right words but didn't speak from their own experience. Because Jesus had experienced God, he spoke of God in such a way that people instinctively sensed, 'Yes, God's like that. That's the truth. This God is important for me. I can't evade this God. He fulfils my heart's desires.'

If you see Jesus as a rabbi within the Jewish tradition, how does your relationship with Jesus change? Imagine Jesus praying the psalms and expressing his experience of God and other people in them. How do you experience Jesus then? How does he strike you? Can you discover unconscious anti-Jewish tendencies in yourself? Are you aware of the Jewish roots of your faith?

Read some of the Old Testament, perhaps the psalms or the first two books, Genesis and Exodus. What do you make of these texts? Do they surprise you because they don't seem very pious? Do you resist, because the Old Testament unsparingly describes life as it actually is, with its heights and depths, confidence and despair, love and hatred, fighting and peace? Have you the courage also to accept the dark sides of God?

2

Jesus the drop-out

Mark hands on a remarkable story: 'Jesus went into a house, and once more such a crowd collected that he and the disciples could not even have a meal. When his relations heard of this, they set out to bring him back by force, for they said, "He is out of his mind"' (Mark 3.20f.).

This scene shows that Jesus' relations with his family weren't untroubled. His family thought that he was crazy. They wanted to bring him home by force. They had the impression that he was damaging their reputation.

The other evangelists didn't include this story. It was clearly too offensive for them. Nevertheless, here historical reality shines through. We can speculate about the deepest reason for Jesus' alienation from his family. Some exegetes suppose that his family was close to the Pharisaic tendency. However, Jesus went round the country as a preacher and miracle-worker. He followed another theological tendency, one stamped more by John the Baptist. Other exegetes think that as the firstborn Jesus had avoided the family responsibilities of the head of the household and that this was why his family wanted to get him back again. They thought that he should be doing his duty at home instead of going round the country preaching the kingdom of God. Perhaps the family was also annoyed that he had gathered twelve unknown men around him and hadn't brought any of them home. In that case this controversy shows the conflict between Jesus' natural family and the apostles, his new family.

Evidently it was difficult for Jesus to detach himself from his family.

Mark reports how his relatives come yet again, this time not to bring Jesus home by force but to speak with him. 'His mother and brothers arrived and, standing outside, sent in a message asking for him' (Mark 3.31). But Jesus wouldn't listen. He looked round and said, 'Who is my mother and who are my brothers?' (Mark 3.33). With this remark Jesus expresses an inner distance from his family – including his mother. Now he has found a new family, the family of those who do the will of God, who hear his words and become open to the kingdom of God.

More than almost anyone else, Jesus detached people from their close family ties. He told one man who wanted to follow him but first to bury his father, 'Let the dead bury their dead: go and proclaim the kingdom of God' (Luke 9.60). Duty to parents comes second to the task of proclamation. God's kingdom is such a powerful reality that it breaks all family ties.

Jesus gives me courage to go my own way, even if my family don't understand it or my friends don't think that it's a good way. That's part of the loneliness in my life. Jesus encourages me to risk this loneliness. It's worthwhile. It makes me open to the mystery of God and God's kingdom.

'God's kingdom' means that God is near. God rules. When God rules in me I'm really free; then I take the form that God has devised for me, that suits me. Jesus calls on me really to go my own way. This unique way which God entrusts to me is more important than any human approval. Every man and woman is unique. That is Jesus' message. And we can all make our own personal way in this world. There is no need to justify this way, to explain it, or to get approval of it from the family We must simply go our own way and do what God tells us in our hearts.

What voices do you hear when you say something, when you meet someone, when you make decisions?

How do you react to drop-outs? Do they unsettle you? Do you reject them or even hate them? Do they bring out hidden longings in you? Do they make you ask how far you really fit in?

Are you ready to go the way that you recognize in your heart as being the right one for you? Or do you want everyone, your family and your friends, to approve of it? Check your opinions and how you behave: are they really yours or are you unconsciously modelling yourself on your parents or people around you, whose approval and recognition is important to you? To follow Jesus means to hear the inner voice, the gentle impulses that are stirring in your heart. If you listen to this voice and hear in it the voice of Jesus, you're being true to yourself and at the same time to God.

3

Jesus the vagabond

Jesus is always on the way. He wanders from place to place. He has nowhere to retreat to: 'The foxes have their holes and the birds their nests, but the Son of man has nowhere to lay his head' (Luke 9.58). Luke in particular has described Jesus as the wanderer. He is the divine wanderer who has come down from heaven to wander among us men and women and to remind us of the divine kernel within us. And on the way he keeps dropping in on men and women to eat and drink with them and to celebrate the joy that comes about when people accept one another and know that they are loved by God.

When I look at Jesus as a vagabond I sense his freedom and the power that goes out from him. He didn't proclaim an itinerant life as an ascetical ideal or make an ideology of it. He simply wandered through the country, meeting people. He spoke to them. He healed the sick when they came to him or when he recognized their distress. He didn't develop any strategy for his preaching or plan any missionary campaign. He went his way in freedom. He felt compelled to go through the villages saying to people, 'The time is fulfilled, the kingdom of God is near. Repent and believe in the gospel' (Mark 1.15). Jesus didn't plan the structures of the church or a consolidation of the national budget, nor did he outline any political vision. He simply wandered in inner freedom, without care and enjoying life. He always had time for anyone he met. Then this person became the most important concern of all. Jesus abandoned any intention of preaching and devoted himself solely to the individual before him. This specific meeting showed that God was near; in it God became visible. By looking at people in a different way Jesus wanted to open their eyes to the nearness of God. Jesus had a clear view of reality. He marvelled at the beauty of nature. He watched the peasants at their work. He saw how things were. And he saw God's activity and God's beauty in everything. He wanted to teach people to see God at work in this way in all things.

No wonder that his family and society had problems with this vagabond. He wasn't bothered about the future. He hadn't married and had a family; he hadn't safeguarded his professional career. He had simply kept wandering. He also proclaimed to others the absence of anxiety expressed in his wandering: 'Do not worry about your life and what you have to eat, and about your body and what you have to wear' (Matthew 6.25). He pointed to the birds of the air and the lilies of the field. They have enough to eat and are clothed in even more beauty than Solomon, of whose great splendour people used to boast.

When I see this Jesus wandering without a care, it dawns on me who God is. Jesus doesn't even have to speak of God. God already shines out in this inner freedom, in which Jesus leaves the Jewish rabbis and their localized teaching far behind. God is the one who frees us from care. In the history of Christianity numerous monks have imitated Jesus the vagabond. During their lifetimes they wandered and didn't settle anywhere. They wanted to wander 'for Christ's sake', to share in his freedom from anxiety and his experience of God.

As cellarer of a monastery I have to look after the people whom we employ, and safeguard the future of the monastery. That seems to be the opposite of the freedom from care lived out and proclaimed by the divine wanderer. But at the same time this Jesus has a great attraction for me. When I go walking on holiday I find Jesus' freedom. But even in the midst of my work I sense something of the freedom that emanates from his wandering. I have no abiding place in this world. All my worries can't prolong my life. I can't gain life, no matter how many precautions I take. Life is to be found somewhere else, in freedom, in an absence of care, in going on. Only those who go on remain alive.

My life is an inward way, a constant wandering. I can't stop and rest. I must wander on. There's an inner necessity, like that felt by Jesus: 'But today and tomorrow and the day after I must go on wandering' (Luke 13.33).

Probably no one in church history imitated Jesus, the carefree wanderer, as radically as Francis of Assisi. He gave away all his possessions. He even took off his clothes in the presence of his own father so that he could wander naked and free through the land. This freedom in wandering brought him an infectious joy. Francis even preached to the birds. In his lack of care he was like the birds of the air who trust God to feed them. Through his life he made Jesus shine out in his own time. People saw in him the face of the free and loving Jesus.

Just try for once to think as you walk around and imagine to yourself that you're wandering free and without a care. You keep going on. You don't stop, but with every step keep wandering. Then you can ask yourself: 'Where do I settle? Where have I found a place? What do I depend on? What robs me of my freedom, inside and outside myself? Am I allowing myself to be ruled by worries or by confidence? What are my basic feelings on my way: fear or trust, worry or assurance, looking after myself or just keeping going?'

Enjoy your wandering! Really look at the beauty of nature and see how your heart feels! Perhaps it will swell with joy!

4

The Jesus who refuses power

Jesus refused all power. Certainly he preached with divine authority, and to that degree he had power over his hearers. But he didn't exploit this power by playing the guru. He cast his spell on people and also called them to be his disciples. Men and women followed him because they were fascinated by him. But he himself had no ambitions to build up a community and dictate which way it was to go.

Jesus had no ambition to rise in the hierarchy of the Judaism of his time, as a Pharisaic rabbi, a scribe or a priest. He also refused all political power. He didn't put himself at the head of a political movement, as the Zealots might perhaps have expected him to do.

When he was taken prisoner by a host of armed men he dispensed with any kind of force. When Peter drew the sword and struck the servant of the high priest, Jesus forbade him to use violence: 'Put your sword in its sheath; for all those who take the sword will perish by the sword. Or do you not think that my Father would immediately send me more than twelve legions of angels if I asked him?' (Matthew 26.52f.). For Matthew, the death of Jesus on the cross is itself a sign of his powerlessness and non-violence. Jesus refrains from translating the divine authority that he possesses into outward power.

Jesus also never exercises power in dealing with his disciples. He never appeals to an authority, but simply says what comes from within him. He doesn't put any pressure on his disciples by giving them bad consciences. He fascinates his disciples. That's why they follow him. But he doesn't tie them to himself. He allows them freedom. When many people don't understand his teaching and turn from him he asks his disciples, 'Do you want to go away too?' (John 6.67). He doesn't adapt his teaching to the expectations of the disciples to make them stay with him. He feels called by God to say what God has entrusted to him, regardless of whether or not his hearers accept it. Jesus refuses to found an organization with himself at its head. He goes his own way, the way of preaching and healing.

I'm impressed by the clarity with which Jesus goes his way. I personally know the temptation to exploit the influence I have on others for my own ends. Today there are numerous stars in church and society who build up fan clubs around themselves. But often enough the stars are devoured by their fans. They're no longer free. On the other hand there are numerous self-styled gurus who bend a community to their will and lead it in an authoritarian way. Often enough they work with spiritual abuse. Those who put the teaching of the enlightened guru in question are threatened with damnation and destruction: 'You'll see where you end up if you don't accept my teaching.'

Jesus resists all these temptations. Perhaps it is precisely because of his renunciation of power that he has exercised so much power down the centuries. Jesus radiates an inner power that casts its spell on people.

Martin Luther King followed Jesus on his way of non-violence. And like Jesus, politically he achieved a tremendous amount. By renouncing violence he had more power than the President of the United States, who was backed by a highly-equipped army. Martin Luther King also preached love to those against whom he demonstrated with his protest marches. This man, who like Jesus renounced all power, fell victim to power. He paid for his non-violent struggle against racial segregation with his life. He was shot by a young white man in Memphis on 4 April 1968.

Where do you exercise power? Do you put pressure on others by threatening to leave, to drop everything, to stop co-operating with them? Are you aware of the power ploys with which you manipulate others and attempt to force them in your direction? Look at the way you behave, the points at which you exercise power over others. Check your words to see whether they come from the vocabulary of power, whether they give others a bad conscience, whether they force people, put pressure on them, drive them into a corner, wound them, disparage and devalue them.

Against the background of your words and actions meditate on Jesus' renunciation of power and allow yourself to be led into the spirit of non-violence by the example of this Jesus of Nazareth.

5

The Jesus who refuses to compete

Many rabbis at the time of Jesus laid down rules about how their disciples should live. And often enough they vied with one another in making the commandments of God stricter and challenged one another by ever greater achievements in fulfilling the law. They weren't interested in social achievements in work and in political organizations, but in achievements before God. The pious were those who achieved something before God, who fasted regularly, said their prayers every day, gave alms, and had something to show before God.

Today many people define themselves in their work and in their family life in terms of what they've achieved. They want to prove their worth by achievement. Jesus gets off this carousel of 'achievers'. He invites people to live. He allows them to be themselves. He tells them that they're loved unconditionally, even if they've nothing to show in return. He turns in particular to those who have no achievements to show: the sinners and the poor, the despised and those without rights. That infuriates the Pharisees, who are proud of the works that they've performed.

Two parables show how Jesus breaks through the spiral of achievement. One, the parable of the labourers in the vineyard (Matthew 20.1–16), infuriates many employers. 'You can't deal with workers and their sense of achievement like this,' they say. Jesus tells of the owner of a vineyard who hires labourers for his vineyard very early in the morning and sends them to work immediately. He does the same thing at the third, sixth and ninth hours. Indeed, he hires labourers once more, at the eleventh hour, just an hour before the end of work, and sends them into his vineyard. When at the twelfth hour he pays the agreed wage, one denarius each, to the labourers he hired last, those labourers who had toiled the whole day expect more. But they too get only the one denarius that they had agreed on as wages.

Here the principle of achievement is turned on its head: 'So the last shall be first and the first last' (Matthew 10.16). What matters isn't achievement and recompense, but faithfulness and reliability in what we do. Jesus doesn't approve of doing nothing. For him work is the sign of a healthy life. But how others assess it isn't important to him. It isn't important to prove oneself through work, to accomplish something that one can be proud of; pride in life is a matter of accepting the work that's offered us and required of us.

In the famous parable of the prodigal son (Luke 15.11–32), the younger brother wants to enjoy life straight away. He takes his share of his inheritance and goes to a distant land – in those days presumably Greece or Italy. There he wants to enjoy life to the full. But in a very short time he's already squandered all his resources. To survive he has to impose himself on a citizen of the land, who sends him to look after the pigs. For Jews, pigs are unclean animals, so this is a humiliation for him. Things get worse and worse, so he resolves to return home to his father. For the day labourers at home are better off than he is abroad, looking after pigs. His father receives him joyfully and gives a party for him, because the son who was dead has come to life, and the one who had lost himself has found himself. However, the older brother, who has been doing his duty day by day, is annoyed about this feast. His anger shows that he hasn't done his work because he enjoyed it, because he got involved in it, but because he expected reward and recognition from it. He reproaches his father: 'I've been working for you all these years and I never did anything against your will; but you never gave me even a kid so that I could have a feast with my friends' (Luke 15.29). The older son had other motives for working: he wanted to buy his father's care, his father's love.

With this parable Jesus is telling us that we don't need to buy God's love with our achievements. That love is already there. God accepts us time and again, no matter what happens. He doesn't attach any conditions to his love, either achievement or conformity. Those who know that they're accepted unconditionally can achieve something in freedom. They're no longer under the pressure of having to prove themselves. They work because they enjoy it, because the work flows out of them.

Jesus shows this inner freedom towards any achievement. But improbably he achieved a great deal in this freedom. In only three years of his public activity he addressed countless people, healed many who were sick and above all set in motion a movement which continues even now and spurs on many people to work for a more humane world. Because Jesus didn't have to prove himself by achieving things, he was free to bring forth fruit a hundredfold, as he himself promises his disciples in a parable. The reason for the hundredfold yield isn't achievement but faith. Faith frees us from the pressure which is a burden on us. So an inner spring can well up in us, and from this spring a great deal of energy flows into the world without our being exhausted by it. For if we don't have to achieve, life can flow, creativity and imagination can blossom in us, and we can accomplish great things.

What do you live by? Do you define yourself by your achievements? Does your life consist in proving yourself to others, and even to God, by your achievements? What's the real motive behind your work, your dedication to others, in your job, in sport, in school, in your religious activities? Does the work flow from an innermost spring in you? Do you enjoy work? Or do you take refuge in work to escape your inner truth, as the older brother did in the parable of the prodigal son?

6

Jesus the friend of women

Mark reports that at the time of the crucifixion of Jesus all his male disciples had fled. But 'there were some women watching from a distance. Among them were Mary of Magdala, Mary who was the mother of James the younger and Joses, and Salome. These used to follow him and look after him when he was in Galilee. And many other women were there who had come up to Jerusalem with him' (Mark 15.40f.).

Here Mark uses the same expression for 'following' Jesus as he does in the case of the disciples. Women were disciples in the same way as men. That was new for the world of the time. In the circle of Jesus' disciples women were on the same footing. What moved Jesus to gather women around him in the same way as men? Evidently as a man he had no fears about coming into contact with women. All the Gospels report that it was the women who had persevered by Jesus' cross. That could by no means be taken for granted. For the Romans crucified relations and friends who grieved around crosses, along with those who had been crucified. They didn't tolerate any sympathizers near crosses. It had probably always offended the male church that the women were the first to be encountered by the risen Christ. Women proclaimed the message of the resurrection to the disciples.

The Greek Luke pays special attention to Jesus' relationship with women. He tells how Jesus on his wanderings was accompanied not only by the Twelve but also by 'certain women whom he had cured of evil spirits and ailments: Mary Magdalene, from whom seven demons had gone out, Joanna the wife of Herod's steward Chuza,

Susanna, and many others. They provided for Jesus and his disciples out of their own resources' (Luke 8.2f.). So when Jesus was wandering around the country, there were always women around him with whom he had a personal relationship. He had healed them, touched them, raised them up, freed them from demons, i.e. from patterns of life which restricted them, from disparaging and condemning themselves. He had restored their dignity as women. And these women weren't just recipients: they also gave something to Jesus in return. They served him not only with their resources, but also with their capabilities, with the inner and outer gifts at their disposal. The Greek word for 'serve' really means serving at table. The women served at table, they served life, they aroused life in Jesus and his disciples. They created a sphere in which life could flourish.

In the house of the sisters Mary and Martha, who have given hospitality to Jesus (Luke 10.38–42), Mary is sitting at Jesus' feet. The phrase used to describe this posture is one typically used of discipleship. It is similarly said of Paul that he had sat at the feet of Gamaliel and had been instructed in the law of the Lord (Acts 22.3). So this woman is just as much a disciple as the other disciples of Jesus. Whereas Martha serves Jesus and his disciples at table, Mary just sits there and listens to Jesus. This annoys her sister. She complains to Jesus and tells him that he should ask Mary to help her. But Jesus takes sides with Mary. She has chosen the good part, which will not be taken away from her. The scene in which Luke portrays Martha shows how open Jesus was in his dealings with women. He claims their hospitality, but he also takes them seriously as disciples. He instructs Mary in what matters most to her. And he joins in the clash between the two sisters without hurting one of them and without allowing himself to be taken over by the other. He makes a clear stand, but in such a way that neither feels scorned.

Yet another scene in the Gospel of Luke seems to me important in shedding light on Jesus' relations with women. The angel by the tomb says to the women who are to be the first witnesses of the resurrection, 'Remember what he said to you when he was still in Galilee' (Luke 24.6). For the angels, the women are witnesses not only to the resurrection but also to the words which Jesus has spoken to them.

Jesus proclaimed his teaching not only to the male disciples but also to the female disciples. They bear witness to his teaching on an equal footing. They hand on his words. They recall these words and keep them in their memories. And as with Mary, these sayings go round and round in their minds, penetrating into them more and more deeply. So the interpretation of the message of Jesus isn't just given by men, but to an equal degree by women. When Luke narrates a scene with a man as the chief character, it is immediately followed by another with a woman in the main role. A parable about a woman is played off against a parable about a man. Luke believes that he can speak rightly of God and human beings only if he does so by speaking about men and women at the same time. Unfortunately the church did not draw any conclusions from this. For too long, only men interpreted the message of Jesus.

The deepest friendship with a woman is that which associates Jesus with Mary of Magdala. Jesus drove seven demons out of Mary Magdalene. She owed him her life. When Jesus died, her world collapsed. But her love outlasted death. Her encounter with the risen Christ is a love story. John describes in the language of the Song of Songs how she gets up early and goes to look for her beloved Lord. In the Song of Songs we read: 'On my bed at night I sought the man whom my soul loves: I sought but could not find him' (3.1). John writes: 'On the first day of the week, in the early morning, when it was still dark, Mary of Magdala came to the tomb' (John 20.1). But she doesn't find Jesus, whom her soul loves. The tomb is empty. However, she doesn't abandon her quest. Three times she complains that they have taken her Lord from the tomb and she doesn't know where they have laid him. The last time she turns to the gardener. But the supposed gardener speaks to her with a word that touches her heart and entrances her, 'Mary.' It's Jesus. Then she turns round. She's completely transformed, and says to him, 'Rabboni' ('My master') (John 10.16). In this word 'Rabboni' she expresses her love for Jesus. Jesus isn't just the master whom many revere, but *her* master, with whom a deep relationship has grown up. He belongs to her. And so she does what the Song of Songs describes as an expression of love: 'I grasped him, would not let him go' (3.4). Jesus allows the contact, but he also puts limits to it: 'Hold me no longer, for I have not yet ascended to the Father' (John 20.17). Jesus is her friend. But his mission goes on. He must ascend to the Father. From there time and again he will come into the midst of his disciples. And he will dwell in the heart of Mary Magdalene. Even beyond death he will live on as her friend.

In the history of Christianity many women have lived as friends of Jesus. Teresa of Avila was encouraged by Jesus the friend of women to take a stand as a woman in what was at that time a misogynistic church. Hildegard of Bingen had the courage to read the riot act to male clergy. She opposed the dictates of the petty-minded Bishop of Mainz and buried someone who had been excommunicated in the cemetery of her convent.

What women strike you as having understood and interpreted Jesus in their own way? What new aspects of Jesus have these women brought out? What have these women understood of Jesus of which too little note has been taken in the official church?

As a woman, what do you feel about your relationship to Jesus? Do you feel that you're noticed and taken seriously?

As a man, what strikes you about Jesus' friendship with women? How have women enriched you? Where have they conjured up new life in you?

7

The Jesus who is capable of friendship

Luke and John have portrayed Jesus as a man who is capable of friendship and gathers friends around him. In Luke Jesus addresses his disciples as friends: 'But to you, my friends, I say, Do not be afraid of those who kill the body and after that can do no more' (Luke 12.4).

Friendship was very important to the Greeks. So the Greek Luke pays special attention to Jesus' capacity for friendship. Luke depicts the earliest community as a Greek association of friends. Evidently Jesus was not only capable of friendship but also made the many people who followed him friends with one another. However, he also had the experience of rivalry among his friends. He strictly forbade this by pointing to his own example. Anyone who wants to be a leader, who wants to go ahead, is to serve. He is to wait at table and serve life. 'But I am among you as one who serves' (Luke 22.27). These words show the role that he chose for himself in his circle of friends.

In the Gospel of John the theme of friendship becomes evident above all in the farewell discourses. There John speaks of 'his own who were in the world' (John 13.1). Here too Jesus calls his disciples friends: 'I no longer call you servants, for the servant does not know what his master does. But I have called you friends, because I have made known to you all that I have received from my Father' (John 15.15). Jesus hasn't treated the disciples as servants but as friends. He has entrusted to them everything that he has heard from his Father, everything that he has experienced in his heart from God. He has shared his most intimate thoughts with them and opened his heart to them. John sees the culmination of Jesus' capacity for friendship in his readiness to die for his friends: 'No one can have greater love than to lay down his life for his friends' (John 15.13).

Jesus' farewell discourses in the Gospel of John are stamped by an intimate atmosphere of friendship. In them we detect formally how the disciples hang on Jesus' words, how sorrowful they become when it becomes clear to them that Jesus is going away from them, that he will be snatched from them by death. He refers to the pain that a mother has in giving birth to a child. But as soon as the child is born, the mother is full of joy. He promises that this will also happen to the disciples. Certainly he will go away from them, but he will return. He will be with them, but in another way. In the resurrection stories John shows how loving Jesus is to his disciples and how their hearts are moved when they have a meal with him and know that 'it is the Lord' (John 21.7).

Time and again the Gospel of John speaks of the disciple whom Jesus loved. He is never given a name. Some exegetes think that he is the author of the Gospel of John. At the farewell meal this beloved disciple reclines 'by Jesus' side' (John 13.23), or, as the Greek really says, 'in Jesus' bosom'. At that time people reclined at meals. They supported themselves on their left elbows and ate with their right hands. The beloved disciple reclines on Jesus' right side. When Peter asks him to enquire whom Jesus is speaking about as the traitor, he leans back and in so doing touches Jesus' breast. Artists have made much of this scene. The beloved disciple is sitting on Jesus' lap. This is an intimate position, the archetype of friendship: artists have expressed their dream of friendship in this image of one person supporting the other, one delighting in the other. Love flows to and fro between them.

In the liturgical tradition of the feast of St John this love is expressed by the consecration of St John's wine at the end of the service. People bring bottles of wine to be blessed and then drink the wine at the family dinner. The wine is also referred to as 'St John's love'. Tradition believed that John was Jesus' beloved disciple and as a result of the love that he had experienced from Jesus he had been more capable of love than any other disciple. Since then many people have been infected by the friendship between Jesus and the disciple whom he loved. Augustine was so fascinated by this friendship that he longed for a similar friendship in his life. 'Nothing can be pleasing without a friend,' he wrote.

Who would you describe as your friend? What kind of friendship do you have? What do you do out of friendship? Are you capable of friendship, or do you just have a lot of contacts? What do you confide to your friends? Do you have the feeling that you can be utterly yourself in friendship? For Jesus the secret of friendship lies in giving his life for his friends. What does that mean for you? What do you give for your friends? Is it something merely external or is it a piece of yourself, your heart, your love, your life? What can you learn from Jesus about becoming capable of friendship?

8

The Jesus who is capable of enmity

Jesus has given offence. He hasn't told people what they want to hear. He has said what God has shown him to be right. This has brought him the enmity of many Sadducees and some Pharisees. The Sadducees saw their religious and economic interests threatened. Jesus had had the courage to overthrow the tables of the money changers and the stands of those who sold doves in the temple and to drive out the merchants and tradesmen (Mark 11.15–19). When the high priests and scribes heard of this 'they sought an opportunity to put him to death' (Mark 11.18). Jesus could also have been more cautious. But God's will was more important to him than people's opinions. And here the issue was the house of God, which should be a house of prayer and not a robbers' den.

The cleansing of the temple is only one image of Jesus' fight against a piety that pollutes the house of faith by dealing with God as if it were running a pious business and using piety for business interests. Jesus consistently acted against this distortion of the relationship with God. By his aggressive appearance in the temple he made the Sadducees his enemies. For them the temple was an important source of income, since the profit from trade in the temple flowed into the coffers of the high-priestly family. So the Sadducees saw their economic base threatened by Jesus' symbolic action and resolved to kill this inconvenient rabbi.

He also made enemies of many Pharisees by criticizing them for their behaviour and castigating them for their hypocrisy. Jesus had many friends among the Pharisees, for many Pharisees were engaged in an honest search. But friendship didn't deter Jesus from identifying and rejecting distortions of piety. His criticism of the behaviour of the Pharisees is often very sharp. Jesus isn't looking for enmity. He does what he feels that he has been sent by God to do. But he isn't deterred from acting by a false concern for the pious. So he keeps clashing with many Pharisees because he doesn't observe all the regulations. He provokes Pharisees by eating and drinking with sinners. He seeks contact with everyone. And he expounds God's law more generously than many Pharisees. However, he doesn't put in question the law that God has given to the people of Israel. He simply wants to clarify its original meaning. The law is to benefit people. Human beings aren't there to observe as many commandments as possible but to live out the image that God has made of them for himself. Jesus shows this by giving two examples. When the Pharisees complain that his disciples have been plucking ears of corn while walking through the fields on the sabbath, something that is forbidden, he justifies their behaviour by saying, 'The sabbath was made for man and not man for the sabbath' (Mark 2.27). This provokes the Pharisees, but they can't object to it. For they sense that the truth is that the purpose of all the commandments is for human beings to be able to live in accordance with their nature.

Some conservative Christians use Jesus' capacity for enmity to justify the way in which they give offence everywhere. But there's also a danger here. If we use Jesus' experience of enmity to justify every conflict in which we get involved, we become blind to our own role in the conflict. Perhaps we give offence because we're incapable of understanding others, and are blind to their true concerns. Some people attempt to claim that their Pharisaism is an attitude of Jesus. When they experience resistance or criticism they hide behind the argument that Jesus, too, wasn't popular with everyone. Such identification with Jesus is always dangerous. It makes us blind to ourselves. I am not Jesus. I am not as transparent and clear as Jesus. So I must first check whether I've got needlessly involved in a confrontation with other people, whether I've simply been stubborn and incapable of understanding them, and whether I've hurt them. Only when I've examined myself sufficiently will I be able to recognize whether the enmity that I experience springs from the other person's hard-heartedness or my own narrow-mindedness.

However, if I remain honest about myself, time and again I will have experiences similar to those of Jesus. If I speak of God's goodness I will be accused of being too lax. If I proclaim Jesus' mercy I will be told that my attitude will land me in hell. Such enmity corresponds to Jesus' experiences. When Jesus speaks authentically of God, he arouses anger and hatred in those with a narrow image of God who feel unsettled by him. Those who speak out will always also encounter enmity. Jesus gives me the courage to show myself as I am, to express myself and my quest for God without seeking to please everyone.

Look at your relationships. Where are you trying to please people? Where do you give way so as not to cause offence? Look at your conflicts. Are you as clear about things as Jesus, or is there also a conflict in your heart? Has the conflict been caused by your clarity and transparency or by a lack of clarity and by ambivalence? Where do you make enemies for yourself unnecessarily because you project your own problems on to them? It isn't always easy to decide whether you're working yourself up into a state of conflict and enmity or whether you have to endure it to remain inwardly clear. Pray to Jesus to make clear to you when you have to make a clean break and expect a dispute, and when you should understand the other person and be ready for compromise.

9

The Jesus who divides

'Do you suppose that I am here to bring peace on earth? No, I tell you, but rather division. For from now on, a household of five will be divided: three against two and two against three; father opposed to son, son to father, mother to daughter, daughter to mother, mother-in-law to daughter-in-law, daughter-in-law to mother-in-law' (Luke 12.51–3).

Those who divide a group are themselves inwardly divided. Those who are reconciled with themselves can also have a reconciling effect on others. This psychological insight suggests that Jesus can't have been a divisive person. For our basic assumption is that he was at one with himself and that he lived in harmony with God. Nevertheless Luke hands down to us these provocative remarks by Jesus.

They are words which challenged the hearers of his time, and perhaps they still cause offence to people today. What does Jesus mean by the term 'divide'? The Greek for this is *diamerismos* (division, split). At this point Matthew has the word 'sword', which is probably more original (Matthew 10.34). For Luke that sounds too violent, so he replaces it with 'division', 'split'. Jesus doesn't call for a division or split. But people are divided about him, because he doesn't fit in. When Jesus speaks, some are for him and others against him. What Jesus says isn't so inoffensive that no one has any objections. He challenges people. And some people refuse to accept his challenge. Jesus announces that this can even split families completely, tear them apart. Jesus thinks it important for everyone to decide for themselves and not out of false regard for others. All should make the fundamental decision about their lives. The important thing is to live one's own life.

Jesus doesn't divide because he's divided in himself. He simply shows up the way in which people are torn apart. He reveals that apparently harmonious families only seem to hold together, that their members have conformed to one another not out of love but out of convenience. But a great deal of aggression has accumulated behind this conformity which rips the family apart internally. Jesus speaks in a provocative way so that everyone can decide for him or against him, so that all can decide on the way that God entrusts to them, so that all can come to life on their own authentically personal ways.

We could emphasize just how provocative Jesus' saying is by calling Jesus a hacker. He throws sand into the workings of big businesses who have networked their computers and think that they now have everything within their grasp. With his love, culminating in his death on the cross, Jesus has crashed the whole software of a society intent only on profit. He is divisive in order that people can at last reflect on what they really want. Jesus is always divisive when he senses that people have erected a firm structure in their lives behind which they hide.

But yet another aspect of the Jesus who divides is important to me: many people haven't ever decided what course to take. They live in an unconscious symbiosis with others, even their own families. They do what others expect of them. Jesus challenges us to seek our own way and to discover our own self. That can happen only if we distance ourselves from the wishes of others. As long as I'm still inwardly bound by such wishes I shall wend my way between conforming to others and doing what I want. And I shall never find myself.

It's only when I stand on my own feet that I can really communicate in freedom with my fellow men and women. Only then can encounter take place. As long as we're entangled with one another and the demarcation lines aren't clear, we can't recognize either the mystery of the other or our own identity. Jesus wants encounters between mature people, independent people. And that first requires division, distancing, detachment. That's the only way to a fruitful relationship.

Are you good at distancing yourself? Or do you prefer to be angry with people who expect things of you? People may have expectations of you, but you're free to decide how far you want to fulfil them. Some people prefer to be angry with others, but fundamentally they're angry with themselves, because they can't distance themselves. Distancing oneself properly can also lead to good and clear relationships. What are your relationships like? Is there a healthy relationship between intimacy and detachment in them? Or are they seething with emotion to such a degree that you no longer recognize yourself? Do you confuse your feelings and needs with those of others? Have you encountered divisions arising out of the division in individuals? Do you divide the people around you? How can you distinguish between a sick and disabling division and the clear break with which Jesus provokes us to authentic life?

The Jesus who reconciles

Jesus' sayings about reconciliation have provoked resistance above all among politicians. The German federal chancellor Helmut Schmidt once famously remarked that the Sermon on the Mount is useless in politics. I want to look at three provocative sayings from the Sermon on the Mount in which Jesus calls for reconciliation.

'So then, if you are bringing your offering to the altar and there remember that your brother has something against you, leave your offering there before the altar, go and be reconciled with your brother first, and then come back and present your offering' (Matthew 5.23).

When I celebrate the liturgy I first have to be clear about my relations with my fellow men and women. If someone there has something against me, I must first be prepared for reconciliation. Perhaps I've unconsciously hurt the other person. Perhaps that person's annoyance with me is simply based on a misunderstanding. I must clarify my relations with my fellow human beings before I can come before God. But what am I to do if the other person doesn't want reconciliation, and is projecting personal problems on to me? I can only do what I can. If others don't want to be reconciled, that's their business.

Jesus challenges me to examine my share in the conflict carefully. Conversation with my brother or sister helps me to clarify where the root of the disagreement lies. Jesus associates worship with reconciliation with one's fellow human beings. I may not dissociate my relations with God from my relations with other people. That's a provocative challenge. My spirituality directs me towards reconciliation with other men and women.

The second saying is just as provocative: 'Come to terms with your opponent in good time while you are still on the way to the court with him, or he may hand you over to the judge and the judge to the officer, and you will be thrown into prison' (Matthew 5.25).

The original Greek text simply reads, 'as long as you are still on the way'. As long as I live and move I must be reconciled with my opponent. This means above all my inner opponent, everything that I fight against in myself, everything that I can't accept. As long as I'm on the way, I am to be reconciled with this inner opponent. I must attempt to accept my shadow sides, which I would much prefer to detach. If I'm not reconciled with my shadow sides, they will bring me before the inner judge, the authority of my own superego. My inner judge will hand me over to the officer, who will torture me with self-accusations and imprison me in my habits. He will throw me into prison, and I will be so shut up in myself that one day it will be too late to break out of this inner prison. As long as I'm on the way it's my task to be reconciled with myself. Only then will I also be capable of being reconciled with the enemies who cross my way.

The saying about loving one's enemy has always met with the greatest approval and the greatest rejection, both at the same time. Some see it as a great merit of the teaching of Jesus; others regard it as a pernicious demand which asks too much:

> You have heard how it was said, You will love your neighbour and hate your enemy. But I say this to you, love your enemies and pray for those who persecute you; so that you may be children of your Father in heaven, for he causes his sun to shine on the bad as well as the good, and sends down rain to fall on the upright and the wicked alike (Matthew 5.43–5).

In loving their enemies, the disciples are to imitate God, who makes his sun rise on the good and the bad. Jesus didn't divide people into the good and the bad. He saw the danger that the good could go bad and he saw the longing for good in the bad. He accepted both kinds of people and showed both of them a way to life. We are capable of loving our enemies only if we first love the enemy in ourselves; if we let the sun of our benevolence shine on the good and bad in us; if we also look gently at those characteristics in us which conflict with our ideal image of ourselves.

Loving our enemies doesn't mean ignoring everything that others do to us. It primarily means not allowing ourselves to be drawn into enmity. If someone fights against me as an enemy, I mustn't react in an equally hostile way. Otherwise the enmity of the other person will become my prison.

My first task is to recognize why the other person regards me as an enemy. Perhaps that person is projecting personal problems on to me. Because others can't accept themselves, they fight against the aspects of my personality that they repudiate in themselves. If I can see that, the other person doesn't become my enemy. I see people longing to be healed and accepted. So I can encounter them in peace. Some people think that loving one's enemies is a great effort. But for me it's far more of an effort to hate one's enemy. For then the enemy determines my own mood and my attitude. For me, loving my enemy means freedom. I don't regard the other person as an enemy but as a human being longing for friendship.

Jesus' saying also has a political dimension. With the command to love one's enemy he sets out to heal the rift that runs through our society and through the nations. Jesus doesn't leave us in peace with hostile stereotypes. He challenges us to use our imagination and creativity, seeking how the different groups in society and peoples at enmity with one another can find another way of getting on together. If peoples on both sides keep on adding up the hurts done to them, the result will be a pernicious and endless conflict, as the situation in the Balkans showed us. All the accumulated hatred is handed on from generation to generation. No military means can guarantee peace unless this potential of hatred is worked through and replaced by reconciliation. Jesus' challenge to love one's enemy seeks to replace the old black-and-white thinking with a summons to new ways of peace and reconciliation.

Are you reconciled with yourself? With what inner enemies must you reconcile yourself? What can't you accept in yourself? Where do you rage against yourself? Try to see everything that bubbles up in you and tell yourself, 'That's what I am. That's part of me. Things can be as they are. I say yes to them.'

Are there people against whom you bear a grudge? What people immediately occur to you with whom you aren't reconciled? With whom would you most like to be reconciled? First look at your feelings. Face the grudge that you have towards the other person and introduce the spirit of reconciliation into this grudge. Perhaps the grudge will then change, and you'll feel a deep peace in yourself. If you're reconciled in your heart with the other person, then consider what concrete, visible steps you can show to indicate the reconciliation. You could seek a conversation, make a gesture of reconciliation or say a prayer of blessing for the other person.

What would you like to do in your particular environment to create an atmosphere of reconciliation? Note how you talk: does this divide or reconcile? Note your thoughts: are they stamped with the spirit of reconciliation?

II

Jesus the free man

Jesus is inwardly free. He does not go by what people expect but solely by the will of God. With his inner freedom he provokes those who are imprisoned in themselves. He expects to engage in conflict with them.

Jesus' inner sovereignty can be seen particularly clearly in the scene about the tax for the emperor. Some Pharisees want to lure him into a trap. They have to concede, 'Master, we know that you are an honest man, that you are not afraid of anyone because human rank means nothing to you, and that you teach the way of God in all honesty' (Mark 12.14). Jesus has clearly given them, too, the impression that he's incorruptible, that he's inwardly free. He doesn't need to judge by human standards, but acts on the basis of his inner feelings. But then they lay a trap for him. They ask, 'Is it permissible to pay taxes to Caesar or not? Should we pay them or not pay them?' (Mark 12.14).

That seems a harmless question. But it was a highly explosive one in the situation of the time. For Jesus would make enemies no matter what he said. If he was against paying taxes to the emperor, the supporters of Herod would denounce him to the Romans. If he was for paying taxes he would have the Zealots against him: they were opposed to paying tax and had a great influence on the people. So if Jesus was for paying taxes, a large part of the people would turn away from him. The Pharisees themselves were undecided. Their understanding of God's law made them reject paying taxes, since God's law didn't justify it. It could only be understood as a harsh stroke of fate sent by God.

However, most Pharisees reluctantly put up with the tax. So their question is an underhand one. They want to lure Jesus into a trap. They themselves are incapable of giving a straightforward answer but expect Jesus to take a clear stand. Jesus' reaction shows that he is so sovereign that no one can drive him into a corner. He doesn't allow himself to be dictated to by the rules of his opponents' game. He doesn't react but acts, and takes the initiative. He sees through the question and says to those who ask it, 'Why are you laying a trap for me? Hand me a denarius and let me see it' (Mark 12.15). Evidently the questioners have a denarius, the coin with which the tax was paid. That, too, shows their hypocrisy. They already pay the tax. So what do they want to know of Jesus? Evidently they're projecting their own problems on to him. Because they pay the Roman tax with a bad conscience, they want to use Jesus to solve their problem. They want to offload their bad conscience on him and drive him into a corner with their question. But Jesus turns the tables with a question in return: 'Whose portrait is this?' They know very well. 'The emperor's.' And now Jesus clinches the matter with his answer, which shows the brilliance of his mind: 'Then pay to Caesar what belongs to Caesar and to God what belongs to God!' (Mark 12.17). What the state gives to citizens, the security of the law, the infrastructure, old age pensions, all this belongs to the state, to the emperor. They are confidently to give the wherewithal for that to him. But as human beings they belong to God. They bear God's image in themselves. So as human beings they are to give to God the worship and honour that is due to God alone.

For me, this answer to the question asked by the Pharisees and the Herodians shows Jesus' absolute inner freedom. Where does Jesus get this sovereignty from? What is the source of his freedom in dealing with people who want to set a trap for him? For me the answer is that Jesus rests in God. He stands firm in God. He lives by another dimension. So people can't touch him.

I would like to share in Jesus' freedom. Like Jesus I would like to avoid the rules of the human game which often enough drive me into a corner. Jesus directs me to God. If I belong to God, no human being has power over me. Jesus doesn't speak about God like those who preached the homilies that I heard in my youth. In them God was used to make me conform, to respect the power of others. Jesus proclaims a God who gives me freedom, who frees me from the grip of others who want to have me within their grasp.

Do you feel inwardly free? Who are the people with whom you feel that you can't really be yourself? Where do you let yourself be driven into a corner? Where do others exert power over you? Think of meeting those with whom you don't feel free. How would the conversation go if you were completely free, if you really spoke your mind, if you didn't allow yourself to be governed by the pressure of other people's expectations? If you've meditated on this freedom, then try to speak in reality as you managed to speak in your imagination. You will see that an encounter with the free Jesus will bring out the freedom that is hidden within you.

12

Jesus the glutton and drunkard

Jesus often accepted invitations to a meal. When he called on the tax collector Levi to follow him, Levi gave 'a great feast for Jesus in his house. Many tax collectors and other guests were with him at table. Then the Pharisees and their scribes, full of displeasure, said to his disciples, How can you eat and drink with tax collectors and sinners?' (Luke 5.29f.).

Luke keeps telling us of banquets in which Jesus took part. Jesus accepted invitations to meals from tax collectors and sinners, from Pharisees and from his friends. The Pharisees were particularly offended that he ate and drank with tax collectors. John, whose school Jesus had attended, was annoyed that Jesus' lifestyle was so different from his own.

John the Baptist was a model for all ascetics. He 'wore a camel-hair garment and a leather girdle around his loins, and he lived on locusts and wild honey' (Mark 1.6). John baptized Jesus. Evidently he regarded Jesus as his possible successor. But when he was in prison, at the same time he was disturbed by Jesus and by his words, which sounded so different from his. Jesus didn't proclaim God's judgement but the imminent coming of God's kingdom, the presence of the merciful and good God. Jesus, who preached about such a gentle God, did amazing things. People told everywhere of how he healed the sick. So John sent messengers to Jesus to ask him, 'Are you he who should come or must we wait for another?' (Matthew 11.3). John directed the attention of John's messengers to what they saw. He claimed that in him the prophecies of the prophet Isaiah were being fulfilled: 'Go and tell

John what you hear and see: the blind see again (Isaiah 29.18), the lame walk; lepers are cleansed and the deaf hear (Isaiah 35.5f.); the dead are raised (Isaiah 26.19) and the gospel is proclaimed to the poor (Isaiah 61.1)' (Matthew 11.5). Jesus knew that it was a scandal for some pious Jews that he didn't fulfil their expectations. So he added, 'Blessed is he who does not take offence at me' (Matthew 11.6).

When the messengers of John had gone back, Jesus compared himself with John: 'John came, not eating and drinking, and they say, He is possessed by a demon. The Son of man has come, eating and drinking, and they say, He is a glutton and drunkard, a friend of tax collectors and sinners! Yet wisdom is justified by the deeds that she has done' (Matthew 11.18f.). Neither John nor Jesus could do right in people's eyes. People protected themselves against the uncertainty caused by John by saying that he was possessed by a demon. They believed that such a harsh lifestyle could only be the result of demon possession. By contrast Jesus, who was hardly notable for his asceticism, but ate and drank quite normally, was taunted as a glutton and drunkard. He was accused of having a lax lifestyle. If Jesus eats and drinks with sinners he cannot be a prophet. The Pharisees took offence at this inner freedom of Jesus. Evidently here their own shadow side came to light. They didn't fulfil the commandments out of sheer love of God but in order to look better to others. Jesus discovers their unconscious aims. God is gracious to everyone. He also has mercy on sinners.

Jesus excluded no one from eating with him. He had meals with the Pharisees. But – and this was completely new in the religious observances of the time – he turned especially to those who were despised. In the Judaism of the time sinners weren't just people who had transgressed God's commandments and were living an immoral life. Among the Pharisees a person was regarded as a sinner simply if he had an occupation that was on their list of disreputable activities. Dice players, usurers, organizers of dove races, and also shepherds, toll collectors, tax farmers, weavers, shearers, leeches, bath masters, tanners and even doctors, shippers, camel drivers and butchers, were automatically sinners. Jesus excluded no one from the kingdom of

God because of their profession or their lifestyle. He preached to everyone the good news that the kingdom of God was near. But the kingdom of God also required them all to repent and rethink.

Jesus didn't need to demonstrate his spirituality by a radical asceticism. He was free to eat or not to eat. He didn't repudiate fasting. But he said that one shouldn't fast demonstratively before others. Jesus was free to go to parties with people who didn't observe the norms of the piety of the time. For me, this too is an expression of the mystery of God. Because Jesus came from God, he didn't have to worry about dealing with people who were regarded as sinners. Because he was clear about this himself, he didn't need to keep away from people who were unclean. He didn't become unclean through having dealings with people who hadn't observed the regulations about cleanness. His cleanness came from his close relation to God. For me Jesus' behaviour is stamped by a freedom from anxiety. He wasn't afraid either of being dependent on eating and drinking or of the people among whom he moved. He was so steadfast himself that he wasn't torn from his centre by contact with others. And he wasn't afraid of the judgement of others. He was free from a desire for recognition and endorsement by the pious or by the established social circles of the time. Because he was anchored in God he could freely do what he thought right.

Look at your eating and drinking. Do you really enjoy it? Or do you just gulp everything down? Do you block out your annoyance, your frustration, your sense of missing something, with food and drink?

Try for once deliberately to eat slowly and to taste every bite, so that you can enjoy God's goodness and loving-kindness.

Can you fast and enjoy yourself? When you do without things and fast, how do you think and talk about the people who don't fast and don't live up to your standards? Do hidden needs and wishes come out? Look at Pope John XXIII. He wasn't an ascetic either. But he radiated a goodness and gentleness that changed the whole church and the world. He understood something essential about Jesus.

13

Jesus the physician

The earliest church called Jesus the 'one and only physician'. The early Christians believed that he alone could really heal. The Bible reports many healings of the sick. People brought their sick and laid them at Jesus' feet for him to heal them. There were also miracle healers elsewhere at that time. But when the evangelists told stories of healings they were less interested in the miracle than in the way in which Jesus dealt with sick people.

Jesus was evidently an experienced therapist. He could diagnose anyone. He calls forward the woman bent double, sitting at the edge of the congregation. He talks to her in a way that draws her out of the isolation in which she finds herself (Luke 13.10ff.). He takes aside the deaf and dumb man who has been brought to him by the people, so that he can give him special treatment. The man has evidently been struck dumb, so he needs a protected space in which he can venture to speak again (Mark 7.31–37). Jesus touches the blind man tenderly. He smears his eyes with spittle and lays hands on him. Since the first treatment isn't completely successful, Jesus lays his hands on the man's eyes once more. Now the blind man can see clearly. 'He was healed and could see everything quite plainly' (Mark 8.25). Jesus knows what each individual feels and how to awaken new life in them.

All the illnesses that Jesus healed can be classified as psychosomatic. They also have a psychological component. Blindness is often connected with our not wanting to see some things. Paralysis has its cause in anxiety: we can't get out of ourselves. We're hemmed in and blocked. The leper can't bear himself. Because he rejects himself, he feels an outcast, completely isolated. Jesus knows that great patience is required before those who reject themselves can accept care from outside. When a leper, probably a man with a skin disease, comes to Jesus and asks him for help, the healing takes place in several stages: 'Jesus had compassion on him: he stretched out his hand, touched him and said, "I will it – become clean!" That same moment the leprosy disappeared and the man was clean' (Mark 1.41f.). Jesus' methods of healing become clear in these two verses.

The first step in Jesus' therapy consists in compassion. The Greek word for compassion really means 'being moved in the gut'. Jesus allows the leper to enter the area of his vulnerable feelings. Then he stretches out his hand. He creates a relationship with the sick person. He doesn't treat him as an object. He offers him his hand and makes contact with him. He embraces him – that's what the Greek word really means. By touching a leper Jesus makes himself unclean. He 'dirties his hands'. He doesn't just see the inner bitterness and the accumulated resentment from the outside. He touches the other person in his leprosy. And anyone who has dealings with people who can't accept themselves will know what garbage one encounters in them. So there are many who prefer to steer clear of such people. They have the impression that they'll be infected by them. Jesus doesn't have this fear. He touches the other person. And then he says, 'I will it – become clean.' Jesus stands by the other person. But now this other person must stand up for himself. Jesus regards him as clean: You may be who you are. But now the sick person too must allow himself to be who he is. In this way he becomes clean. We could translate the Greek word *katharistheti*, 'Be who you are: clean, pure.' Don't confuse your feelings with self-rejection, resentment or bitterness. Be completely yourself. Live out the image that God has made of you for himself and don't falsify it. Stop spoiling the image by those negative thoughts that you keep having of yourself.'

Jesus never treats sick people as passive objects. He says to the paralysed man, 'Arise, pick up your stretcher and go home' (Mark 2.11). The paralysed man is chained to his stretcher by fear. He's afraid of being unsafe. He's hemmed in, blocked. The others could see his fear. They could see how he went red when he began to speak, how he trembled and sweated. So he preferred to remain lying down.

Jesus doesn't treat him but challenges him. With a challenging remark he confronts the man with his own will and his own strength: 'You can stand up. Just try. You can do it.' The sick man is to put his stretcher under his arm. The stretcher is a sign of his insecurity, his paralysis, his inhibitions. He would love to stand up if he knew that from now on he would be secure. Jesus assures him that, insecure and inhibited though he is, he can get up and go his way. As a physician Jesus doesn't take all the responsibility. He arouses in the sick person an awareness of what he can do for himself. Jesus reinforces his will, so that now he no longer seeks to blame others for his illness, and doesn't even look to them for help, but takes responsibility for himself.

Where do you feel like a leper, insufferable? Where can't you accept yourself? What paralyses you, blocks you and inhibits you? Where are your blind spots?

Offer your leprosy, your paralysis, your blindness, your exhaustion to Jesus. Talk to him about your illnesses. What happens to you then? What could be the causes of your present state?

What Jesus did then is now being carried on by physicians and psychologists. Jesus gave the gift of healing to all who believe in him. You too can have a healing effect on others. You can raise them up if they're bowed down. You can accept them if they reject themselves. Where are you being looked for today with your capacity to heal? Do you radiate healing, or bitterness and depression? Watch out today for what radiates from you.

14

Jesus the family therapist

As we've already seen, Jesus didn't have a harmonious family history. Part of his family even rejected him because of his public activity. Jesus' personal history made him sensitive to relations between parents and their children. He could see the way in which fathers and mothers were hurt by sons and daughters. So Jesus became one of the first family therapists.

The Gospels know the four classic relationships in which people can be hurt: the relationships between father and daughter (Mark 5.21–43), between mother and daughter (Mark 7.25–30), between father and son (Mark 9.14–29) and between mother and son (Luke 7.11–17). Here Jesus never heals just the son or the daughter but always also the father or the mother. His therapy is free of reproaches. He doesn't judge and he doesn't evaluate. He simply unravels the pernicious entanglement of parents and children so that each can find his or her own self.

Mark tells us how a father brings to Jesus his son who is possessed. The demon hurls the boy to and fro, so that he writhes on the ground. Jesus first asks for the history of the illness: 'How long has he had that?' (Mark 9.21). Jesus immediately recognizes that the son's sickness is connected with the father's attitude. Evidently the father was afraid of aggression and sexuality and therefore attempted to drive these out of his son. So the son had no space in which he could deal appropriately with these two important energies in life. He worked out the suppressed aggression by gnashing his teeth and in fits, physically directing his anger against himself and against his father. The son's suppressed sexuality had often hurled him into the fire and almost burnt him to death. The father asks Jesus in his helplessness, 'If you can, help us; have pity on us' (Mark 9.22). Jesus first turns to the father and points out his lack of faith in his son: 'If you can, those who believe can do anything' (Mark 9.23). The father recognizes that he has never really believed in his son. So he begs in tears, 'I believe, help my unbelief!' (Mark 9.24). Jesus frees the father from his entanglement in fear and by pointing to his faith sets him on his feet. Only then does he turn to the son and the unclean spirit which has disturbed the son's thoughts and feelings: 'I command you, you dumb and deaf spirit: leave him, and never return to him again' (Mark 9.25). He frees the son from the destructive patterns of life which have him in their grip. He takes him by the hand and celebrates resurrection with him.

In the father-son and mother-daughter relationships Jesus heals the son and the daughter by driving the demon, the unclean spirit, out of them. Jesus has recognized that the children have been demonized because their parents have never seen them as they really are. The parents have projected their own suppressed passions on to them. Or they've offloaded their unsatisfied needs and wishes on to them.

The son is to study what the father never dared to do. The daughter is to have every opportunity for the further education that the mother was refused. Such projections impose themselves on the son and the daughter like demons, like unclean spirits. The projections distort their view of what they really are and confuse them. Jesus heals the sons and the daughters by ridding them of their baneful spirits and helping them to be themselves.

In the father-daughter and mother-son relationships the healing takes place only after son and daughter have died. In the transference across the genders a symbiosis comes about which is so strong that it can be dissolved only through death. Only then can Jesus put the son or the daughter on their own feet. There is a father who is the president of a synagogue. Perhaps the sheer importance of his position has made him overlook his own daughter. The daughter draws attention to herself by falling sick and refusing nourishment. In his helplessness the father turns to Jesus: 'My daughter is on the point of death. Come and lay your hands on her, so that she may regain her health and her life may be saved' (Mark 5.23). While Jesus is going down the road with him, he is told that his daughter has already died. Here, too, Jesus turns first to the father: 'Don't be afraid, only believe' (Mark 5.36). The father has been clinging to his daughter out of fear. Now he must learn to let go of her, to leave her to God and herself. Only if the father has let go of the daughter can Jesus take her by the hand and raise her up. She stands up and walks around. Now she goes her own way. Jesus gives orders for her to be given something to eat. She is to feel herself, to look after herself, to feed herself.

Jesus treats the fathers and the mothers differently. He sees that the fathers are anxious for their daughter or their son. That's their problem. So he tells both fathers to believe. If they believe in the good at the heart of their daughter or son, they can let go of them and leave them to develop in their own way, without having to control and regulate everything. The mothers' problem isn't fear, but a failure to distance themselves. Jesus distances himself from the Greek mother who asks him for help over her sick daughter (Mark 7.24–30). The mother learns from Jesus' attitude that she must distance herself from her daughter. Jesus confronts the mother weeping over her dead son with herself (Luke 7.11–17). She is to stop weeping for her son. She is to come to herself. Then she will see how her son raises himself up and finally dares to say what he thinks in his innermost being. As long as she clings to him weeping, he cannot live.

Jesus' knowledge of family therapy becomes evident from the way in which he turns to the father and the mother, the son and the daughter. He knows all the complications in the relationships between parents and children and unravels them. He knows about the fear of fathers and the tendency of mothers to take their children over completely, forgetting themselves in the process. He encourages both to be themselves.

Jesus heals the wounds that we've received in our relationships and makes it possible for us to discover our own sense of life. Only if we're reconciled with the history of our hurts will we find our own way, will we live out what is within us. Look at your relationship with your own father and mother against the background of these four biblical relationship stories.

What has wounded and hurt you? What was difficult in your relations with your parents? What positive roots do you owe to your parents? If you look at the history of your own life with its hurts and its healthy roots, what traces do you discover that lead you to life? What mark do you want to make on this world? If you're a father or a mother, look at your relationship with your children. Are you repeating what you experienced? What children are you overlooking, what children are you using for yourself? Offer your children to Jesus, for him to heal the hurts that you've done to them.

15

Jesus the exorcist

When Jesus spoke for the first time in the synagogue of Capernaum the people reacted dramatically: 'And his teaching made a great impression on them, because unlike the scribes, he taught them with (divine) authority. And a man was sitting in their synagogue who was possessed by an unclean spirit. This began to cry out, "What have we to do with you, Jesus of Nazareth? Have you come to destroy us? I know who you are, the holy one of God"' (Mark 1.22–4).

Jesus speaks of God in a way that impresses people. They simply can't let his words pass them by. But Jesus' words also bring out the unclean spirits in people. When Jesus speaks, the truth of a person appears. People have to take a stand. And the demons in them are also stirred up. All the demonic images of God that have previously held them captive are brought to light. It becomes evident that we often want to use God solely for our own ends. God has to correspond to the images that we've made of him. When Jesus speaks, we can no longer hide behind our images of God. Our false perspective is shown up. The unclean spirit that has made its home in us stirs. It blurs our image of God and dirties our image of ourselves. We see ourselves in the wrong light. We see everything in a distorted way through the spectacles of our own suppressed passions and needs. When Jesus speaks of God, we have to take off our spectacles. We're challenged to see properly. But we resist, since this disturbs us. It spoils the rest that we've made for ourselves.

Described in our present-day language, demons are obsessions, fixed ideas, complexes, emotional confusion, blocks in our thinking, an inability to think clearly, a split inside us. I know the reaction of the man who cried out when Jesus was preaching. When I speak in lectures of God's mercy one of the audience may react aggressively. He tells me to go to hell. I'm surprised that he attacks me so sharply, since I certainly haven't attacked him. But evidently a demon is speaking in him, repressed aggression, unconscious feelings of hatred, bitterness and fear.

When Jesus spoke of God in the synagogue of Capernaum he didn't moralize, threaten or hurt anyone. But evidently there was someone there who had misused God as a kind of security system. He went into the synagogue to dissociate himself from godless people and put himself above them. He used God for himself. Jesus speaks of God in such a way that people can never use God for their own ends. Jesus' words make me decide whether I rely on God or whether I bring down God to my level.

Jesus doesn't react to the demon's cry by arguing with him but by commanding him: 'Be quiet and leave him' (Mark 1.25). Jesus doesn't deal mercifully with the demon. He casts it out. He frees the man from the evil spirit that holds him captive. So the man can think clearly again. The demon once again hurls him to and fro and then leaves him with a loud cry.

The people are amazed: 'Here is a teaching that is new, and with authority behind it; he gives orders even to unclean spirits and they obey him' (Mark 1.27). But the scribes are opposed to this new teaching. They make accusations about Jesus: 'He is possessed by Beelzebul; he casts out demons with the help of the leader of the demons' (Mark 3.22). That's the most subtle defence against being unsettled by Jesus. We project our own demons on to him and say that he himself is demonized. But Jesus continues to speak about God in such a way that people are divided over his words. Those who accept his words not only acknowledge God but also see themselves in the true light, and in Jesus' words see their own way to life.

What demons stir in you when you hear Jesus' words or when you read how Jesus casts out demons? Do you have demonic images of God, the image of the God of vengeance, the capricious God, the competitive God?

Are there unclean spirits in you that disturb your thinking? Do you have the right image of yourself? Or have you painted over it a picture of yourself that falsifies your original image?

When you look at your fellow men and women, what distorts your view? What spectacles are you wearing?

Jesus lures the demons out of their hiding place in the unconscious. What does Jesus bring out in you? Where does he unsettle you and make you feel insecure?

16

Jesus the ghost

Jesus feeds five thousand people who have been listening to him all day with only five loaves. After this miracle he gets his disciples into a boat so that they can sail to the other shore. There he will be safe from Herod's minions. Jesus is evidently afraid that popular enthusiasm about this miracle will cause King Herod to pursue him. While his disciples are steering for the safety of the other shore he withdraws to a mountain to pray.

Late in the evening the boat is on the lake. A strong, cold east wind, the kind that fishermen on Lake Gennesaret fear, blows up. When the wind suddenly rises, it's impossible to make progress against it. The disciples row in vain. Jesus, praying by himself on the mountain, sees their distress and comes to meet them on the water. 'And about the fourth watch of the night he came towards them, walking on the sea. He was going to pass them by, but when they saw him walking on the sea they thought it was a ghost and they cried out, for they had all seen him and were terrified. But at once he spoke to them and said, "Trust me, it is I! Don't be afraid." Then he got into the boat with them and the wind dropped. They were utterly and completely dumbfounded' (Mark 6.48–51).

Matthew adds to his narrative that when Jesus spoke, Peter had the courage to get out of the boat and walk over the water to Jesus. But he became afraid and began to sink: 'He cried out, "Lord, save me!" Jesus immediately stretched out his hand, grasped him and said to him, "O you of little faith, why did you doubt?"' (Matthew 14.30f.).

We can no longer say precisely what happened that night. Certainly the experience that the disciples had of Jesus the ghost was a deep one. We must guard against interpreting this story only metaphorically. The disciples had gone on the lake at night often enough and had experienced all kinds of dangers there. But evidently that night they had a miraculous encounter with Jesus which took away their fear.

What the disciples experienced then is at the same time an image of hope for us. It isn't just a matter of seeing Jesus as the miracle-worker who can do anything, who even breaks the laws of nature. Were we to do that, we would be steering clear of Jesus as a supernatural being. This Jesus who walks on the lake at night also enters our night. He comes to us when we risk drowning in the storms of life.

The lake which is stirred up by a storm at night is an image for the nocturnal storms in our subconscious, for the storms we get caught up in when all external security collapses, when we lose our job, when our marriage breaks up, when an illness throws us out of our safe boat.

The fourth watch of the night suggests the mid-life crisis, in which the unconscious is often stirred up. The ground on which we stand begins to shake. Unknown forces break out in us and threaten us. When we're trapped in our fear, we don't even recognize Jesus. The disciples think that he's a ghost. He terrifies them. They cry out. Jesus doesn't always come to us in the night as someone who is loving and tender. In the night we also see the night side of Jesus. Then he appears as a spirit who terrifies us. We don't understand him. We can't fit him in.

In the midst of our fear and confusion Jesus says, 'Trust me, it is I! Don't be afraid' (Matthew 14.27). Perhaps such a word of trust also enables us, like Peter, to get out of the security of the boat and venture on the water. But as soon as we get fixated on the storms within us, we go under. Jesus still appears to us today in the nights of our fear. He appears to us in our dreams. But often enough we don't recognize him. In dreams he doesn't appear in a familiar form, but like a ghost, an appearance, a figment of our imagination. Sometimes Jesus encounters us in a dream as a pursuer who terrifies us. But if we turn to him and speak with him, he reveals himself to us as the one who protects us, who accompanies us on our way, who gives us confidence and strength.

We aren't alone. Jesus goes with us, even over the water, even to inaccessible places. He goes with us through the night of our life. That's an experience of Jesus which gives me courage. It's the unknown Jesus whom I cannot grasp. But it's the Jesus who says of himself, 'It is I.' This 'It is I' echoes God's revelation of himself to Moses. 'I am here. I am who I am.' In Jesus God himself is there. I believe that he rescues me from all tribulation.

How's your boat? Is it sailing through waves and breakers? What storms are tossing you to and fro? Imagine the situation of the disciples in the boat and see how far it corresponds to your present situation. And then invite Jesus to come into your night and get into your boat. But perhaps you must first get out of a boat that has become too narrow, the boat of your ego, so that you can row through the storms yourself with all your might. Perhaps you've become unsettled because you've kept God out of your boat, because you believed only in your own strength. When Jesus gets into your boat, peace comes, and you can confidently continue the journey through the waves of your life.

17

Jesus the wild man

The American Franciscan Richard Rohr wrote a bestseller entitled The Wild Man. *Richard Rohr gave many lectures to groups consisting solely of men who were in search of their identity as males. Since Rohr found many American males conformist and powerless, he presented them with the image of the wild man.*

The wild man doesn't conform. He's free. He's full of power. He stands up for himself. He supports men on the way to their manhood. The wild man isn't macho. He's integrated his anima, his feminine side. He doesn't experience his masculinity in opposition to women, but as someone who is aware of a woman's own worth and finds her a life-giving and fruitful source. I can write about Jesus as the wild man only if I have the opposite to the wild man in view. Anselm of Canterbury calls Jesus 'our mother'. And in an edifying early Christian book Jesus appears to a woman called Priscilla in female form to communicate a revelation to her. The Acts of Thomas, an early Christian work, calls him 'the polymorphic Jesus'. So if I see Jesus as a wild man, at the same time I think of his feminine aspects. Otherwise I get a one-sided image of Jesus.

We've domesticated the masculinity of Jesus often enough. The Jesus of the images of the Nazarene in the early nineteenth century is sexless. In these images we miss the male force. But when we read the Gospels, we're met by a powerful Jesus. For me, the story in Mark 3.1–6 is a good example of Jesus the wild man. Among his hearers there's a man 'who had a withered hand' (Mark 3.1). The man has conformed. He has held back the hand with which he could intervene in events, for fear of getting his fingers burnt. He's given up any attempt to take his life into his own hands, to shape and form it. With four hands we touch one another. The man refuses his hand to the men and women around him. He has no relationships; he's incapable of relationships.

Round the man sit Pharisees, watching to see whether Jesus will heal on the sabbath. For that was allowed only when there was the gravest danger to life, and not in the case of this harmless illness. Jesus isn't intimidated by the phalanx of Pharisees. He commands the man with the withered hand, 'Get up and put yourself in the centre' (Mark 3.3). He is to give up his marginal position and put himself where he belongs, at the centre. He is to learn to stand up for himself before others. And he is to learn to discover his own centre.

Then Jesus turns to the Pharisees. He isn't afraid of them. He confronts them with his question, 'What is allowed on the sabbath, to do good or to do evil, to save a life or to destroy it?' (Mark 3.4). It's a provocative question. For this question indicates that Jesus doesn't see the correct observance of the narrow sabbath regulations as the fulfilment of God's will, but as something evil. For him it's wicked to pass by someone in need. If I overlook others with their hurts in order to do what is supposed to be God's commandment, I destroy life. I'm serving death, and not life.

Now Jesus looks round the Pharisees one by one. He turns to each of them, but the Pharisees give way. They hide behind a wall of silence. Jesus looks at the Pharisees 'full of anger and sorrow over their hardened hearts' (Mark 3.5). In his anger, Jesus dissociates himself from the Pharisees. He doesn't allow himself to be torn apart by anger, but uses the anger as a force to set himself apart from the Pharisees and escape the spell of their power. In his anger Jesus says to each single Pharisee: 'You may be what you are. But that's your business. You may have a hardened and dead heart. But that's your problem. I do what my heart commands me. I give you no power. You're there and I'm here. I won't allow you to tell me what I may or may not do.'

Jesus shows not only his anger but also his sorrow. The Greek here is *syllypoumenos* ('having compassion', 'feeling for', 'sorrowing with'). Jesus feels with the Pharisees. He senses what has died in their hearts. That makes him sad. Jesus grieves with the Pharisees. He understands them. And in his sorrow he stretches out his hand to them. He doesn't want to cut his links with them. But they won't accept his hand. They remain stuck in their harshness, in their stubbornness. Jesus has made them an offer, but they don't accept it. So Jesus does what his heart tells him. He says to the man, '"Stretch out your hand." He stretched it out and his hand was made whole again. Then the Pharisees went out and with Herod's supporters resolved to kill Jesus' (Mark 3.5f.). The life of the sick and conformist man is more important to Jesus than his own. He risks his life to heal the life of this man.

The wild man shows his greatness by putting his whole existence at stake so that life can win. But with their resolve to kill Jesus the Pharisees confirm what he has seen in their hearts: they are inwardly dead and therefore want to kill the one who gives life. They show that their piety is hard-hearted and destroys life instead of healing it. The wild man in Jesus also comes out in the woes against the Pharisees. Jesus is completely uninhibited here. We can sense how the words flow powerfully out of him: 'Woe to you, scribes and Pharisees, you hypocrites! ... Woe to you, you are blind leaders! Woe to you, scribes and Pharisees, you hypocrites, you are like whitewashed tombs that look handsome on the outside but inside are full of the bones of the dead and every kind of corruption' (Matthew 23.15–27).

Jesus hasn't told people what they want to hear. He's expressed his feelings. And often enough his words are full of force, but also full of anger. His anger isn't a sense of personal injury, but always divine anger against any falsification of the image of God, against the misuse of religion and against spiritual bigotry. With his strong words Jesus is provocative, so as to disclose the truth in people.

Take the scene in Mark 3.1–6 as an image of your relationship with people. If you're offended by a colleague, imagine telling him or her, 'You're you and I'm me. You may be who you are. I'm not criticizing you for being like that. But I shall do what I want to do. I'm me and you're you.' And then try, like Jesus, to feel with your colleague. What is he feeling? What is she suffering from? Why do they act like this?

Do you accept both sides in you, anger and sorrow, aggression and tenderness, wildness and warmth?

18

Jesus the foreigner

In some parables Jesus has painted a self-portrait. The self-portrait which fascinates me most is the story of the Good Samaritan. A man is going down from Jerusalem to Jericho. On the way he's attacked by robbers. They steal his clothes, his money, all his possessions. They half kill him. Doubled up with pain, the man is lying injured in the dust. A priest is going along the road. 'He saw him and passed by' (Luke 10.32). A Levite does the same thing. A Samaritan, a foreigner, someone who was suspect to the Jews, an 'outcast', sees him and has compassion on him. He pours oil and wine on his wounds, binds them up, and puts him on his donkey, to take him to an inn. In this Samaritan Jesus paints a image of himself.

Jesus is a foreigner. He isn't the typical pious Jew. He comes from Galilee, which seemed suspect to the Jews. Pagan tribes had also settled in Galilee. They had mixed with the Israelite population and were no longer pure Jews. The Samaritans were despised even more by the Jews than the Galileans were. The Samaritans were descendants of the Asiatic tribes which had been settled in Samaria after the Israelites had been carried off to exile in Assyria. They had accepted Yahweh religion; however, they didn't worship Yahweh in the temple in Jerusalem but on Mount Gerizim. Jesus identified with this Samaritan. He comes from another world, not the familiar world of pure Judaism.

In the person – man or woman – who has fallen victim to robbers and is lying plundered and half dead by the wayside, Jesus paints a image of us. We've been hurt by our life history. We're full of wounds inflicted by our fathers and mothers. People have robbed us. They've sapped our energy. We've given them everything. Now we've nothing but ourselves. We're lying in the dust and can't get up again. The Greek word for human being, *anthropos*, comes from the verb *anatrepein*, which means 'hold up something, raise something'. Our life has prevented us from walking upright. Now we're dependent on the compassion of others if we're to have ground under our feet again. The representatives of religion and its cult pass us by. Jesus is the Samaritan, the foreigner, who went down from Jerusalem to Jericho, from the holy city to one of the oldest cities in human history. Luke portrays Jesus for us as the divine wanderer who comes down from heaven to visit us human beings where we live. The Greek word for visit is *episkeptein*. It means cast an eye on something, look something over, inspect it. So Jesus comes down from heaven to see how things are going with us. He looks at us and sees us lying robbed and injured by the wayside. He doesn't pass me by when I'm wounded, as the priest and Levite did. Full of compassion, he bends over me and pours oil and wine into my wounds.

Jesus, the messiah, the anointed one, anoints our wounds with oil. Oil is a symbol of the healing power of Jesus. The wine is an image of his love. Jesus binds up our wounds, raises us up and puts us on his donkey.

Van Gogh painted a marvellous image of the Good Samaritan. The image quivers with effort. The Samaritan is making a supreme effort to get the wounded man on to his donkey. The church fathers interpreted this scene to mean that Jesus lays us and our suffering on his shoulders to raise us to the cross and set us upright. On the cross Jesus dies upright, outstretched. Van Gogh, who himself suffered greatly from his inner divisions, probably understood more than anyone else what it meant for Jesus to raise up the man lying in the dust, to raise him from the dust as it were like Adam, and to create him anew.

Jesus paints a fine self-portrait here. In this portrait Jesus approaches us in his undistorted sensitivity. In the two thousand years since then, countless men and women have made efforts to accept those who've been robbed and injured, those who've been overlooked and are lying on the roadside, to go to them and raise them up. From this image Mother Teresa drew the strength to turn to the men and women lying in the streets of Calcutta, uncared for by the representatives of either state or religion. In her something of the image of Jesus has shone out in our time.

The image of the good Samaritan has also asked too much of many people who believed that they had to drag the wounded around with them all their lives. But Jesus paints a more humane image. It's enough to bring the wounded person to the next inn and leave him there. The innkeeper, probably an image of God, will then care for him. Jesus has picked us up and carried us to the cross, so that raised up there we can go our way once more. We need bear one another only to the next inn. We aren't therapists who can heal all wounds. We go part of the way with the wounded and bring them into the saving sphere of God, so that they are healed.

Who has wounded you and plundered you? Where are you lying half dead by the wayside? Imagine Jesus coming to you and pouring oil and wine into your wounds. Allow Jesus to raise you up.

Jesus painted the portrait of the Samaritan to invite us to act as he does. Where are wounded and plundered people lying on the wayside of your life? To whom should you go today?

19

Jesus the bread

In his novel And Never Said a Word, *Heinrich Böll tells of the poverty of the Bogner family, who live with their three children in one room. Their poverty is contrasted with the wealth of the childless Franke couple. Mrs Franke is a leading light in church circles. Every morning she goes to communion and receives the body of Christ. But that doesn't make her sensitive to the poverty of Katy and Fred Bogner. On the contrary, she lords it over them. Frau Franke receiving the body of Christ is contrasted with the reverent way in which the Bogners treat bread. In the poverty of the post-war period Katy Bogner knows the value of the bread that feeds her and her children. For Böll bread is a symbol with almost magical connotations. In the daily bread something becomes clear of Jesus, whose words touch Katy's heart and feed her in the midst of her poverty.*

Bread stands for all that we hunger for; it stands for what feeds us, what we can live on. Bread strengthens us for everyday life. When wandering through the wilderness the Israelites hungered for bread. And God himself gave them bread to eat. He made manna fall from heaven. The Israelites satisfied their hunger with manna on the way through the wilderness. Jesus was bold enough to call himself the bread that satisfies our hunger: 'I am the bread of life: whoever comes to me will never hunger' (John 6.35). This claim was a provocation for the Jews. Jesus uses the term 'bread' of his own person. He claims that he can satisfy our deepest hunger. A woman like Katy Bogner in Böll's novel understands this saying. She has an idea that something goes out from this Jesus from which she can draw hope in her poverty.

Whereas the watery homilies preached in church leave her cold, her heart is touched by the 'husky song of a Negro which penetrates everything ... and he never said a mumbling word ... and never said a word'.

Jesus compares the bread that he is with the manna that the Israelites ate in the wilderness. They ate the manna, yet they died. 'But this is the bread which comes down from heaven: if anyone eats it he will not die. The bread that I shall give is my flesh, for the life of the world' (John 8.50f.). In the midst of the wilderness Jesus claims that he can feed us. In the wilderness of poverty, in the wilderness of inner emptiness, in the chaos of feelings, a word of Jesus can be nourishment that allows us to travel on. Katy Bogner experienced that. 'When I lie awake at night and weep, when everything is finally silent, I often feel that I get through. Then nothing matters to me, house and dirt, even the poverty; even the fact that you're away doesn't matter to me.' When Jesus' word touches her, when she senses Jesus' presence, she is fed in the midst of the wilderness, she experiences life in the midst of death.

Jesus identifies the bread that he distributes with the flesh that he gives for the life of the world. He becomes the bread that feeds us precisely where he hangs helplessly on the cross. It's a provocative paradox: the dying man becomes food for the living. And yet this paradox matches our experience. If someone gives himself for us, unconditionally, as Jesus did on the cross, we can live by it; then it's food for us which supports us in all the distress in our life. On the cross Jesus is as it were baked for us in the fiery oven of suffering. It's love that makes him the bread that feeds us. In the end of the day our longing is always to love and be loved. Jesus who loves us to the end on the cross – as John puts it in his Gospel – satisfies our longing. In his unconditional love for us he becomes the bread that feeds us with our lack of the experience of love.

Many people stuff themselves with food so as not to feel their lack of love, in order to suppress their annoyance and their disappointment. But they find out that this never works. The hunger for life and love keeps announcing itself again. Jesus says of himself that whoever comes to him and follows him will never hunger again. Those who know that they're loved unconditionally by Jesus stop filling their bellies in order to conceal their emptiness. Jesus didn't just claim to be the bread that feeds us. He also gave us the eucharist as a sign of this statement. There in the bread he gives us his own body, which he sacrificed for us. So the bread in the eucharist becomes the sign of the love with which he loved us to the end on the cross. By eating this love incarnate in the eucharistic bread we discover that Jesus himself is the bread that satisfies our hunger. Jesus says: 'He who eats my flesh and drinks my blood has eternal life' (John 6.54). Eternal life doesn't primarily mean life after death, but a life in which time and eternity already coincide now, in which heaven and earth touch each other and God and human beings are reconciled with one another. Sometimes on receiving the eucharistic bread I've had the experience of everything coming together as one. I sense that now in the middle of my journey I'm already at the end. Now God's infinite love flows through my body. Now there's real life in me, eternal life, which can't be destroyed even by death, because it's steeped in the divine life and the divine love.

What really feeds you? What do you live on? What strengthens you on your way to freedom? What is your deepest hunger, your deepest longing? What satisfies your hunger? How do you fill your void?

What experiences have you had when receiving communion? Do you experience Jesus as the bread that comes down from heaven? What images occur to you when you eat the eucharistic bread? What is the deepest experience that you've had on receiving the body of Christ?

20

Jesus the water of life

For those who are wandering in the wilderness, water is the embodiment of life, refreshment, regeneration. In many religions water is a symbol of the power to purify and renew body and soul. When we wash with water we don't just cleanse ourselves from external dirt. Rather, we wash away all the stains that obscure our original and pure image. Many fairy tales tell of the spring of youth. Those who drink from it remain young. Water symbolizes spiritual fertility. The spring from which fresh water wells up is an image of the inexhaustible energy of spirit and soul.

At the time of Jesus, the Jews had their own feast for celebrating the mystery of water. It was the Feast of Tabernacles, celebrated six months after Passover. This was originally a harvest festival. It was celebrated in the open air. People erected booths. In the night they celebrated with lights the pillar of fire which had gone ahead of the Israelites on the exodus from Egypt. In the morning they then went to the spring of Siloam in a solemn procession. Water was drawn there with a golden pail, and the procession moved through the Water Gate back to the temple. The high priest held up the golden pail of water for a while and then poured the water into a great bowl, from which it flowed down various channels deep into the ground. This rite was meant to recall the miracle of water in the wilderness. When the Jews rebelled against God because they risked dying of thirst, at Yahweh's command Moses smote the rock. Then fresh water flowed out of the rock.

After this sacred action by the high priest during the Feast of

Tabernacles, Jesus proclaimed that what the high priest had done happened through him:

> Let anyone who is thirsty come to me. Let anyone who believes in me come and drink. As scripture says, 'From his heart shall flow streams of living water.' He was speaking of the Spirit which those who believed in him were to receive; for there was no Spirit as yet because Jesus had not yet been glorified (John 7.37–9).

Jesus is the water of life. In his death on the cross he will pour out the water of the Holy Spirit on all men and women. On the cross his heart will open, and blood and water will flow from his pierced heart. That's an image of the Holy Spirit, which becomes a spring of sparkling water. Those who believe in God will have their hard hearts broken open. A spring will well up in them that will never fail, because it's a divine spring.

Jesus had already applied the image of the living water to himself in his conversation with the Samaritan woman. Whoever drinks the fresh water which comes from the deep well of Jacob will certainly thirst. The water that Jesus gives becomes in the one who drinks it 'a flowing spring whose water gives eternal life' (John 4.14).

Water refreshes. Water purifies and renews. All life springs from water. Fairy tales know the water of life that can heal the sick king. In many cultures water has feminine connotations. What kind of experience did people have when they identified Jesus with the water of life? Evidently they experienced Jesus' words and his person as a refreshing spring. Jesus doesn't supply stagnant water. Those who encounter him become new, come into contact with their own liveliness, from which life springs up.

Jesus' teaching is like the water of the womb in which a baby swims and on which it feeds. Water can develop a tremendous force. Floods show the untamed power of water. Lao-tse says of water: 'There is nothing softer, nothing more unstable in the world than water. And there is nothing more powerful; it can bend even the strong and stubborn. It cannot be compelled, because it adapts to everything.'

Those who encounter Jesus can't hide behind their rigidity any more. They are made to move. Their rigidity is freed up. An encounter with Jesus has a quality of its own. We say of authoritarian people that they petrify us. By contrast, we get the impression that other people are completely invisible. We don't even see them. If I offer my hand to someone, I sense either power or clarity or warmth – or perhaps nothing at all, because the hand has no contours. When people experience Jesus as water they find that Jesus adapts himself to everyone, assimilates to them without losing his own contours. Just by grasping my hand completely, he loosens up all that is rigid in me. All formality ebbs away. I'm asked a question. I have to take a stand. All masks dissolve in the water. What's authentic remains. And I sense in myself a spring that never fails. I won't dry up. I will never be exhausted. For the spring that wells up in me through Jesus is inexhaustible, because it's divine.

Try this exercise. Close your eyes and imagine that you're sitting by a clear spring or a bubbling mountain stream. How does this make you feel? What memories emerge? What comes to life in you, what begins to flow? Or take the image of the rock in the wilderness which Moses strikes. All at once water flows out of it with which the thirsty Israelites can still their thirst (Exodus 17.1–7). What's rigid and hardened in you? What's dried up in you? What would you like to break out in you? Are you in contact with your inner source? In baptism you had water poured on you so that your life would never dry up, but you would always know of the inner source which wells up in you incessantly, because it's divine.

Can you imagine Jesus with his refreshing way of speaking of God and human beings bringing you into contact with your inner sources? Expose yourself to his words. Perhaps then something will come to life in you which had been dried up for a long time.

21

Jesus the light

Light expresses a primal longing in human beings, the longing for life and happiness. We say of a loving person that he or she is the light of our life. Light is an image of knowledge and illumination. People have always longed for illumination. This longing was widespread above all in Gnosticism: 'There must be more than everything.'

We mustn't just look on the surface, but see reality, the primal ground of all being. Buddhism teaches its adherents to see through the appearance of the real and recognize its very essence. In this longing for light and illumination Jesus says, 'I am the light of the world. Whoever follows me will not go around in darkness but will have the light of life' (John 8.12).

Here Jesus is telling us that he brings light into human darkness. Wherever he is, the world grows brighter. Those who dare to rely on him don't fumble around in darkness; they aren't disorientated, but their life becomes brighter and happier.

Jesus shows that he is the light of the world through a sign. He heals the man born blind. The man born blind is an image of our state. From birth onwards we don't see through things. We go through life blind. We don't want to see our own reality. We prefer to soothe ourselves with our illusions about life. Jesus begins his treatment of the blind man by spitting on the earth. Then he makes a paste with the spittle and smears it over the blind man's eyes (John 9.6). Finally he sends him to the pool of Siloam, to wash himself in it. When the man returns he's been healed. He can see again.

Two motifs are expressed in this healing story. One motif is the earth. Jesus applies clay to the blind man's eyes to tell him, 'You've been taken from the earth, and only if you accept your earthiness, your inner dirt, can you see.' To see means to see one's own truth, especially its unacceptable side. The Latin for earth is *humus*, from which comes *humilitas*, humility. Those who in their hybris refuse to see their own reality become blind. Only those who have the courage to descend into their own humanity can open their eyes and see what they truly are.

The second motif is the encounter with Christ. Siloam means 'the one who has been sent' (John 9.7). In the pool of Siloam the blind man encounters Christ, the one sent by God. For John that is an image of baptism. The early church understood baptism as illumination. Faith means seeing anew. Those who believe see deeper; they see reality. They see through things, down to the depths. They see everything as it really is. They stop looking through the dark spectacles of their pessimism or the rose-coloured spectacles of their attempts at repression. Both images, the clay and the dough, point to a new creation of human beings by Jesus. Jesus restores people to what the Creator meant them to be. He frees them from the blind spots with which they have darkened the glorious form that God intended for them in creation.

Jesus' saying about the light expresses the experience that John and his community have had of him. It's the experience that people dare to have near Jesus: they open their eyes. Then everything becomes plain to them. They no longer fumble around in the dark. They're illuminated by faith. They see the inner light that God has put in everyone. They don't sink into the darkness of their depression.

Jesus' words and Jesus' behaviour radiate light. The dark horizon becomes bright. Through his words Jesus brings light into the darkness of our thoughts and feelings. All at once everything becomes clear to us. We see into the depths of things. We recognize the truth of all being and we know our own truth.

Do you know your blind spots? What do you find difficult to look at with open eyes? What if you had the courage to look at the whole truth about yourself? Would that liberate you?

What people can you say are lights of your life? Who has brought light into your darkness? At baptism, the child receives a candle. In it we express the thought that the world becomes brighter and warmer through every child. Can you believe that you too are a candle, bringing light and warmth to your surroundings? For whom might you be a light?

*If you look at Jesus under the image of light, what does that illuminate in you? In Buddhism those who meditate seek illumination (*satori*). Have you ever found that all at once everything becomes clear, that you 'see through', that you know the foundation of the world?*

22

Jesus the good shepherd

*With the image of the good shepherd Jesus expresses the deep longing of men
and women in the ancient world. The Jews saw God as the true shepherd who
leads his people. At God's command Moses was the shepherd and leader of his
people. The Greeks knew of the shepherd who stands in a large garden and
carries a sheep on his shoulder. The garden recalls paradise. The Greeks
associated their longing for a whole world with the shepherd. For many cultures
the shepherd is a caring father figure, an image of God's fatherly care for men
and women.*

*The early Christians took over the longings of Israel and Greece. Like God,
Jesus is the shepherd who leads his people to life. The Greeks associated the
figure of the good shepherd with Orpheus, the divine sinner. His song tamed
wild animals and restored the dead to life. He is usually depicted in an idyllic
landscape surrounded by sheep and lions. Orpheus also appears again among
the early Christians as Jesus. Jesus is the divine singer who with his words
tames the wildness in us and restores the dead to life. When in the Gospel of
John Jesus calls himself the good shepherd he addresses all the images of
shepherds that slumber in the human soul as archetypical images of salvation.*

Jesus says of himself, 'I am the good shepherd. The good shepherd
gives his life for the sheep' (John 10.11). The mark of a good shepherd
is his readiness to give his life for his own. Jesus puts himself before
his disciples. He takes their place. He hurls himself into the breach
so that no wolf can tear the flock apart and no robber can penetrate
the fold. As shepherd he goes to his death for them. By his death on
the cross he wards off all danger from the sheep. The cross becomes

an insuperable obstacle for all the wolves that want to get into the fold.

Jesus says something else about himself as the good shepherd: 'I am the good shepherd; I know my own and my own know me, as the Father knows me and I know the Father' (John 10.14f.). Jesus knows every disciple personally. Every individual is important to him. He calls each of them by name. There is an intimate relationship between the shepherd and his sheep. Jesus loves his sheep. In this remark we can hear the motif of Orpheus, who entranced people with his songs. People have always attributed love songs to Orpheus. The shepherds were thought to sing of love. It's no coincidence that Christmas songs are often shepherd songs. The Christmas concerti of Corelli, Manfredini and Torelli use the melodies of Sicilian shepherds. The love that Jesus has for his own resounds in these shepherd melodies. In these songs he touches the hearts of his followers with his love.

In Matthew and Luke Jesus describes his behaviour as a shepherd in the parable of the lost sheep:

> Which one of you with a hundred sheep, if he lost one, would fail to leave the ninety-nine in the desert and go after the missing one till he found it? And when he found it, would he not joyfully take it on his shoulders, and then, when he got home, call together his friends and neighbours, saying to them, 'Rejoice with me, I have found my sheep that was lost' (Luke 15.4–6).

As a good shepherd Jesus goes after the lost sheep. He lovingly puts the confused and exhausted animal on his shoulders. We people are like sheep which have gone astray in the scrubland of life. Jesus looks for us because we're important to him. And he celebrates a joyful feast when he has found us. The hundred sheep are also an image of our wholeness. We've lost our centre, our wholeness, ourselves. As the good shepherd Jesus goes after all that we've overlooked, suppressed and lost. He finds all that is scattered in us and feasts with us to celebrate the fact that we've become whole, become ourselves.

If you have a picture of the good shepherd, look at it again closely. What feelings does it evoke in you? What are the longings on which this picture is based? What notion of Jesus does it evoke in you?

In the twenty-third Psalm we say, 'The Lord is my shepherd, I shall lack nothing.' For Immanuel Kant that was the deepest experience of his faith. The intellectual philosopher sensed something else in this verse of the psalm. In it his heart found rest. Perhaps this sentence just sounds beautiful to you, but passes you by. Yet if it's really true, how do you experience your loneliness, your lack of care and love? Do you long to be able, like Kant, to build on this statement that as the good shepherd Jesus leads you to a pasture in which you find life?

23

Jesus the door

In many fairy tales the door plays an important role. In the castle there's a door that has to remain closed. The lord of the castle (Bluebeard, for example) gives his young wife keys for all the doors. There's just one door that he forbids her to open. But the prohibition itself arouses her curiosity. So she opens the forbidden door and is terrified to see many murdered women in the room behind it. The prophet Ezekiel mentions the closed door of the temple through which no one may go, because God himself entered through this door (Ezekiel 44.1–3).

Doors often occur in our dreams. There are dreams in which we can't find the door to our house. Or the door is shut and we've forgotten the key. Such dreams indicate that we've lost access to ourselves. We aren't in touch with ourselves. We can't enter the house of our life. We're shut out of our innermost being.

In his discourse about the good shepherd who in contrast to the thieves and robbers goes in to the sheep through the door, Jesus describes himself as the door: 'I am the door; whoever goes in through me will be saved; he will go in and out and find pasture' (John 10.9). Jesus claims that he is the door for us, through which we find access to life. In his saying he is addressing a human need. He recognizes that people aren't in touch with themselves, that they've lost access to their true being. By his words he wants to open the door so that they find the way to their true being and to God.

Jesus promises us that those who go in through the door will be saved. They will be healed and made whole. They will find themselves. They will make contact with themselves. And they will go in and out. The door opens and closes. It opens up a way in for me, into my inner house. But it also lets me go out. The door shows the link between inside and outside. And only those who live both inside and outside can have a healthy life. Those who live only inside shut themselves off from the outside world. They remain unfruitful. Those who live only in the outside world become superficial. They lose themselves. It's going in and out that keeps people alive. Jesus is the door. Through him we find access to ourselves. But he also drives us out of ourselves, so that we go into the world and shape it.

The door is a metaphor for the transition from one sphere to another, from this world to the other world, from the profane to the holy. In some religions there is the door of heaven, which represents the transition to the divine sphere. Jesus is the door through which we not only go into ourselves but enter the house of God, through which we come to God.

In the Middle Ages Christ was depicted as lord on the portals of Romanesque churches. He decides who shall go to heaven and who shall go to hell. Through him we enter the church, the holy sphere. He is the real access to life. Those who go through Christ, the door, enter the sphere of life, the divine life; they're already in heaven now.

In the Revelation of John the image of the door is supplemented by the symbol of the key: 'Here is the message of the holy and true one who has the key of David, so that when he opens, no one will close, and when he closes, no one will open' (3.7). The key opens the door to the mystery for us. In myths and fairy tales, to possess the key often means to be initiated into the mystery, to gain access to the mystery. Jesus is the key that initiates us into God's mystery. He opens the door to us so that we can enter God's sphere and be at home in God. And Jesus is the key that opens up access to ourselves, to the mystery of our true humanity.

Sometimes I have an inkling of the reality of these metaphors of door and key. Something dawns on me in my encounter with Jesus. Then a door opens for me, and I enter the sphere of the authentic, the truth, the sphere of God, the only place where I really find myself.

What doors are closed in you? What doors lead you to life? Have you already found the key to yourself? What were the key experiences through which something dawned on you? Can you remember important doors that you've been through, doors that have opened for you, doors to people, doors to new possibilities? Look at the person of Jesus, his behaviour, his words, his way. Does Jesus become a door, a key, that opens up access for you to the mystery of your life and the mystery of God?

24

Jesus the vine

Jesus says of himself, 'I am the true vine' (John 15.1). In the Greek the adjective he alethine ('the true') stands after the noun ('vine') for emphasis. In this saying Jesus wants to tell us: 'I bring about what you see in every vine. If you look carefully enough, then my relationship to myself will dawn on you; then you will know who I truly am.' Jesus fulfils the archetypal image of the vine. If we concentrate on the vine, we recognize in it who Jesus is.

In the end of the day, what Jesus says of the vine is true of all that is. All that is earthly is an image of the mystery of Jesus. Doors fulfil their nature in Christ. Bread first shows in Christ what is in it. Jesus isn't unworldly. If we look at the world with our eyes open, we shall discover an image of Christ in everything. In every farmer who sows seed and reaps the harvest, in the grain of mustard seed, in the leaven, in the vine, in every builder who builds a house, in every teacher who teaches children, we have an idea of who Jesus is and what his humanity means.

In the Bible the vine is an image of the people of Israel. God himself is the vintner. He tends his vine. In Israel the vine was also regarded as the messiah's tree. In Greece the vine was a symbol of the fullness of life. It was consecrated to Dionysus, the god of intoxication, ecstasy and the transformation and renewal of all life. When Jesus calls himself the true vine, he claims that he is fulfilling all the longings that people have ever associated with the vine.

Jesus above all associates two images with the vine. First there is the inner connection between the vine and the grapes. This is an image of the intimate relationship that Jesus has with his followers. The believers are the grapes hanging on the vine. They receive their juice from him. Without the vine the grapes don't come to maturity. They wither and drop off. The juice of life flows into the grapes from the vine. Those who remain attached to the vine have a fruitful life. Jesus expresses that in the image of abiding: 'Whoever remains in me, with me in him, bears fruit in plenty' (John 15.5f.).

I recognize in myself a longing for my life to be fruitful. Sometimes I'm horrified when I meet people in whom everything is dried up, with no life, no fruit. But I'm well aware that they can't produce fruit by themselves. Fruit will grow in them only if they remain in contact with the vine, if once again the spirit of Jesus flows into them as spirit that gives life and bears fruit.

The second image is that of the wine which gives our life a new taste. The wine is the blood of the earth. The Greeks regarded it as the blood of Dionysus. Wine is the elixir of life, among the Greeks even the drink that bestows immortality. In Islam it's regarded as the drink of divine love and as a symbol of spiritual knowledge. At the beginning of his activity Jesus transformed water into wine at the marriage in Cana. Through his incarnation our life is transformed. It no longer tastes like stagnant water, but like wine that delights the human heart. The church fathers compared the six jars of water that were transformed into wine at the wedding in Cana with the three jars which became wine at the feast in honour of the Greek god Dionysus. Jesus fulfils the longing that the Greeks associated with Dionysus, the longing for intoxication and ecstasy, the longing for fullness of life. Ambrose summed up this Dionysian longing by speaking of the sober drunkenness of the spirit which Jesus gives us. What Jesus did at the beginning of his activity comes to completion at his death. There Jesus consummates the marriage which he has begun with us in his incarnation. John says that in death Jesus loved us to the end. Jesus wants to be the wine that intoxicates us, that fills us with love and joy. That's a different way of understanding himself from that of the ascetic who only gives us a bad conscience. There are people in whose presence one hardly dares eat anything, let alone drink wine. Jesus' radiance is different. He gives himself and his love in wine.

One of my brother monks once asked in a sermon how different Jesus would taste to us had he said, 'I am a slimming camomile tea.' Had he done so we would associate him with something else: asceticism, a preoccupation with ourselves and our health, self-pity, caution. Jesus wants to be a source of ecstasy, sweetness and flavour for us. Above all, he wants to give us the taste of love and joy and not the pallid taste of rightness and correctness.

When you're in love, presumably you drink wine with your beloved. What happens to you when you sip the wine? What taste does it leave behind in you? Can you remember a wine that particularly enchanted you, that made love stream right through your body? The early Christians associated such experiences with Jesus.

25

Jesus the way, the truth and the life

In the farewell discourses before his death Jesus utters the memorable saying 'I am the way, the truth and the life' (John 14.6). Not only have philosophers and theologians reflected on this statement and discussed it; it also moves many people who don't understand it. This saying of Jesus plucks at their heart-strings. The question is how they arrive at the experience that Jesus had of God which enabled him to formulate such a saying.

In handing down this saying John has created a reality that we can't go back on. A saying once spoken is like a wave that keeps going until it has reached every level of our soul and every region of this world. Jesus' saying discloses to us the mystery of our true humanity.

'I am the way.' In all religions the way is an important symbol of human life. Human beings are wanderers. They're always on the way. They mustn't stop. They keep travelling on. They have a destination. The destination is life and knowledge. But the routes to it are often long and winding. They lead along by-ways and wrong turnings, through thickets and along narrow paths. When the people of Israel wandered in the wilderness, Yahweh went at their head on the way to the promised land. Yahweh carried his people on the way like a son. Nevertheless the people didn't believe in the Lord, 'who went ahead of you on the way to find you a camping ground' (Deuteronomy 1.33). Similarly, Jesus goes ahead of the disciples 'to prepare a place for you' (John 14.2). Jesus goes before us to prepare a camping ground for us in heaven. Jesus is the way to God. Those who rely on Jesus – John tells us – will find their way to life and to God. But this way isn't always a convenient one. It can become the way of the cross for us, a way which 'crosses out' our own intentions and requires us to bear the burden of the cross. And often our way leads through a labyrinth of winding paths until we find the hidden spiritual centre, our true self, and in it God as the centre of our life.

'I am the truth.' When Jesus calls himself the truth, we must keep in mind the Greek notion of truth. Truth, the Greek for which is *aletheia*, means that the veil that lies over reality is taken away and that we see reality unveiled, as it really is. The Greeks were troubled that reality seemed to be veiled to them.

We see everything only as if it were under a veil. We don't know reality. Jesus claims to take away this veil that conceals reality. Those who understand Jesus see through it. They see through to the foundations. They recognize reality as it comes from God. They come into contact with the primal ground of all being.

But Jesus also leads me to my own truth. When I meditate on Jesus' words, they also take away the veil that I've drawn over my whole personal reality because it's unacceptable to me. Jesus leads me into the abysses of my soul and discloses them to me. Jesus says that the truth makes us free. 'If you abide in my word you really are my disciples. Then you will know the truth, and the truth will make you free' (John 8.31f.). Those who run away from the truth about themselves are pursued by the fear that the truth will catch up with them, that others will discover what lies behind their façade. In the encounter with Jesus I can't hide myself. In it my truth is disclosed. But this truth will make me free. It will lead me to true life.

'I am the life.' We all long for life. But each of us understands something different by life. For some, life means experiencing as much as possible, travelling as much as possible and seeing people. For others, life consists in liveliness, in a new quality of life. For yet others life means living wholly in the present moment, an intense sense of themselves and everything around them. Jesus calls himself the life. He claims that he is fulfilling our longing for life and liveliness. He says that we first experience what life is through him.

In the prologue to the Gospel of John we read, 'In him was life, and the life was the light of men' (John 1.4). And in I John the author says of Jesus, 'For the life was made manifest' (I John 1.2). Jesus sums up his message in his saying, 'I am come that they may have life and have it more abundantly' (John 10.10). What experience lies behind these words? Evidently the disciples experienced Jesus as someone who radiated life. He wasn't a boring preacher; life flourished in his presence. When he spoke, something moved, something came alive in his hearers. And once they listened to his words, they knew what life really meant. Jesus has come that we may have life in abundance. In him the meaning of life becomes evident. Life means more than experiencing a lot. We have real life only when life streams into us. And for John life can flow into us only because it participates in *the* mystery of life, divine life.

Today, deliberately follow the ways you have to take towards God. Where are you going? What does it mean to go, to be on the way?

What does life mean to you? When do you feel alive? What do you need to live? What helps you really to live?

What is truth for you? Do you face the truth about yourself or do you run away from it? Where have you experienced the veil being lifted so that you simply see what is there? In such moments you touched on the truth. You looked into its very foundation. Everything became clear to you.

26

Jesus the resurrection

What is life? Jesus answers this fundamental philosophical question with a remarkable statement: 'I am the resurrection and the life. Whoever believes in me will live, though he dies, and whoever lives and believes in me will never die' (John 11.25f.). This is an almost incomprehensible remark: Jesus – the resurrection. Those who believe in him arise from death to life even now; they have already passed over from death to life.

John thinks that many people are alive and yet are dead. They aren't really alive. They live only on the surface. But those who believe in Jesus, who understand who this Jesus really is, rise now from the tomb of their fear and self-pity, from the tomb of their paralysis and their inhibitions, their darkness and weakness. Resurrection takes place in the midst of their everyday life. They arise from narrowness into a broad space, from darkness into light, from rigidity into liveliness.

John tells us a story to show what Jesus means by saying 'I am the resurrection.' Jesus raises up the dead Lazarus, who has already been lying in the tomb for four days. His feet and hands are wrapped in strips of linen; his face is veiled with a linen cloth. He is lying behind a stone and is already stinking. Those who lie behind the stone of a lack of relationships are cut off from life. For them everything rots away. Everything takes on a bad smell. They have a cloth over their faces. They're only a mask. They have no authentic life. They're bound hand and foot. They aren't really free. Resurrection means Jesus' words of love reaching his friend through the stone. A loving word brings the friend to life. It loosens the binding that wraps him up and constrains him. It frees him from the mask behind which he hides himself. The resurrection of Lazarus makes it clear that the one who believes in Jesus will live, even if he dies. Love will prevent him from falling victim to death. Love is stronger than death. It penetrates any stone and loosens up all rigidity. Our bodies may die in death, but not our true selves. Love reaches beyond death into eternal life. In faith we have now already passed from death to life, from rigidity to liveliness, from a lack of relationships to love.

The saying about Jesus being the resurrection came back to me when I was reading Dostoievsky's novel *Crime and Punishment*. Dostoievsky prefaced his novel with the biblical text of the resurrection of Lazarus as a motto. Sonya, whose poverty has driven her to prostitution, reads out this story to the murderer Raskolinkov. In the novel she herself then becomes Jesus, who calls forth Lazarus from his tomb. With her love she loosens up the rigid heart of the murderer and awakens love in him. She transforms the prisoner with no relationships, who is surly to his fellow captives and rejects them, into a loving human being. I think that Dostoievsky is very bold in embodying the figure of Jesus in a woman. Sonya, the prostitute, lives out the mystery that Jesus is the resurrection. Dostoievsky writes of Raskolnikov: 'He had risen and he knew it; he felt it completely with his new being, but she – she lived solely in him.' When through love a woman awakens a man to life or a man awakens a woman to life, resurrection takes place; then it becomes evident what Jesus means with his saying, 'I am the resurrection.' For Sonya, Jesus was the source of her love, and she wasn't deterred by the years of the murderer's rejection and harshness. She sensed the power of the resurrection in Jesus' love and thus became capable of awakening to life and love the man without relationships, caught up in himself.

Look at your life: where is your real life, and where is there just emptiness and routine? What makes your life worth living? Where have you experienced resurrection in your life? What has roused you from rigidity to life? What has brought you out of the tomb of your fear and resignation? Where have you risen out of your lack of relationships? Perhaps you haven't thought of Jesus in connection with any of these experiences of resurrection. But — the Gospel of John tells us — if you rise to life from the tomb you encounter Jesus, even if you don't see him, even if you don't think of him. If resurrection takes place in your life, then Jesus is in you and Jesus rises in you.

27

Jesus the friend of children

*Mark reports a scene in which children come to Jesus and he blesses them:
'People were bringing little children to him, for him to lay hands on them. But
the disciples abruptly drove the people away. When Jesus saw this he was
indignant and said to them, "Let the little children come to me; do not stop them.
For the kingdom of God belongs to such as these. Amen, I tell you, anyone who
does not welcome the kingdom of God like a little child will never enter it."
Then he took the children in his arms: he laid his hands on them and blessed
them' (Mark 10.13–16).*

The disciples think that children would only distract Jesus from his
real concerns. So they send away the people who've brought their
children for Jesus to bless. The disciples are rooted in a Pharisaic way
of thinking. The Pharisees are lacking in humour and have no feeling
for children. They think that playing with children is a waste of time
for the pious and prevents them from attaining the world to come.
They value children only as descendants. It isn't proper for a rabbi to
pay attention to children.

Jesus sees things differently. He becomes indignant and angry
about the attitude of his disciples. He's furious at them for driving
away the children. Whenever Jesus becomes angry he shows just how
nonsensical the attitude is of those with whom he gets cross. Whereas
the Pharisees discussed whether children had any part at all in the
kingdom of God, since they had no works of the law to show, Jesus
uses the child as an example of how we stand with God. We don't get
a share in the kingdom of God by fulfilling commandments but by

becoming small, childlike, conceding that we always stand before God empty-handed.

What does it mean to accept the kingdom of God as a child? In dreams a child is always a symbol for the pure and original, the new that will be born in us. To accept the kingdom of God, to make room for God in ourselves, at the same time means becoming wholly ourselves, casting aside the roles and masks that we think we have to put on before God. Just as Jesus takes the children in his arms, so we are to make contact with the child in us. In us there's the hurt child who has been overlooked, struck, insulted. And in us there's the divine child, the source of creativity and liveliness, of originality and authenticity. When we take the hurt child into our arms, it stops crying and preventing us from living. It can be just itself, helpless, wounded, abandoned. Through the hurt child we discover the divine child in us, the child that was always in us and has shown us how we can get through all perils and hurts.

Jesus blesses the children by laying hands on them. The hurt child in us needs a protective hand. Jesus' blessing is like a protected space in which the children can feel looked after, cared for, relaxed. In this protected space the wounded life in us can flourish.

Jesus makes time for the children. He doesn't teach them, because he sees in them what is original, pure and straight in human beings. He holds his hand over the pure and original image of God in us, in protection and blessing. Jesus also blesses the hurt child and the divine child in us, drowning the voice of the superego which sounds so rational and wants to tell us that there are more important things to do than to deal with the child that is in all of us.

When did you last dream of children? Were the children in your dreams sick, hurt, neglected? Try to make contact with the wounded child and the divine child in you. Talk to the child in you. With Jesus be an advocate for the child in you, but also for the children around you, who perhaps sometimes make you nervous. They want to show you something important about the way that you have to take. Particularly if you have a great sense of self-importance, children will show you up and direct you to the child in you that's crying out for attention.

Are you good at getting on with children, or do you think that playing with them is a waste of time? Can you manage to make them happier, to understand their deepest intentions and insights? Do you let children tell you things? Do you allow yourself to be taught by them?

28

The Jesus who is tempted

The Letter to the Hebrews says of Jesus: 'We do not have a high priest who is incapable of feeling our weaknesses with us, but one who has been tempted in all things like us, but has not sinned' (Hebrews 4.15).

The author of the letter to the Hebrews, an educated theologian, sees the humanity of Jesus in the fact that like us he has been tempted and assailed. Jesus doesn't stand above everything. He knows from his own experience that it's impossible to be human without being tempted. The experience of temptation enables Jesus to feel with us. The Greek word here is *sympathesai* (from which our word 'sympathy' comes). Jesus is sympathetic with us because he is one of us, because he suffers with (*syn*) us, because he has shared our experiences and our sufferings.

Three of the four Gospels report the tempting of Jesus. Mark simply says briefly that the Spirit drove Jesus into the wilderness after his baptism and that Satan tempted him there. Matthew and Luke describe three archetypal temptations which also endanger the process by which we become ourselves. These three temptations make it clear that Jesus recognized the danger into which his vocation as an itinerant preacher had led him. Any vocation can be misused. The higher a person's spirituality and calling, the further he or she can fall. The more popular someone is, the greater the danger that he or she will be devoured by their fans and be prevented from living out what they feel in their innermost being. Jesus saw the perils of his mission very clearly. He spent forty days thinking about them. For him that was a time of struggle. Afterwards he was mature enough to devote himself to his task without distorting it by selfish purposes.

The first temptation comes when Jesus is hungry after fasting forty days in the wilderness. 'Then the devil said to him, If you are the son of God, command this stone to become bread' (Luke 4.3). This is a temptation to consume everything that's on offer. Everything is to serve to satisfy my hunger. I don't help people because they're important to me and need help, but because I want their attention. I give a lot because I need a lot. Some people turn every 'stone' into 'bread' that is to satisfy their hunger, their own needs. They turn their work, their success, their possessions, the people with whom they spend time, into recognition, praise, sex, love, simply in order to satisfy their own needs. Jesus doesn't succumb to this temptation. He doesn't use people for his own ends, but turns to them because it's good for them. Jesus resists the temptation by pointing to another form of nourishment: 'Man does not live by bread alone' (Luke 4.4). Human beings live by God, the word of God. If I have my foundation in God, I can give a great deal without wanting a great deal. I can give because I have, because God's spring wells up in me.

In Luke, the second temptation is power: 'I will give you all the power and splendour of these kingdoms, for it has been handed over to me, for me to give to anyone I choose. Do homage, then, to me, and it shall all be yours' (Luke 4.6). This is the fundamental temptation that everyone knows, the temptation to have power over others. For we all know our own helplessness. We feel helpless towards some people, helpless towards our own mistakes and weaknesses, helpless to resolve some conflicts. Power is the promise that we will get a grip on everything, so that we will never seem weak again, so that we will belittle others in order to believe in our own greatness. We know these power-plays well enough. We know where we can hurt others. For where we insult and wound, we have power over others. This is destructive power. We attain it by falling down before the devil and worshipping him. So in the end we're also serving an idol. We think we have power, but in reality we're possessed by power. Power has us in its grip.

Thomas Mann has given an impressive description of this in his novel *Doctor Faustus*. In it the German composer Adrian Leverkühn makes a pact with the devil so that he can always compose brilliant music. But the price that he has to pay for his genius is love. He will never again feel love in his life. Those who subscribe to power lose their capacity to love. Their love becomes empty and cold. The warmth that only love can give vanishes from their lives.

The third temptation relates to the image of God. The devil invites Jesus to prove in public that he is son of God by jumping down from the pinnacle of the temple. The angels of God will protect him. That's probably the greatest temptation for spiritual people, to misuse their spirituality so that they can see themselves as special and present themselves to the outside world as having this special quality. Such people have often really had deep spiritual experiences. But then they begin to behave as if they were God. That exercises a strong fascination on many people, which they find it difficult to escape. Jesus resists this temptation. He knows that he is God's son. But he is also fully human. He wants to encounter men and women as one of them and to tell them of God, not to lord it over them. He doesn't want to draw attention to himself. He wants to proclaim the word of God. He avoids the temptation to misuse the spirit to which many spiritual gurus succumb today. They promise people spiritual experience, but at the price of unconditional obedience to their persons.

What fascinates me about Jesus is that he knows these human temptations, that he has really experienced them, but hasn't succumbed to them. As someone who has been tempted, Jesus is close to me. I know that he understands me. There are temptations that make us stronger. The early church father Antony, a monk in the Egyptian desert, learned this: he compared temptations to the storm that makes the tree dig its roots deeper into the ground. But there are also temptations which endanger our humanity. These are the three typical perils that Jesus withstood in the wilderness.

Do you recognize these temptations in yourself? What is your greatest temptation? Do you sometimes want to exploit everything for your own ends: other people, your work, creation, God?

Where does power exercise a dangerous fascination over you? Do you know power-plays by which you put pressure on others in order to make yourself look great?

The most dangerous temptation is to use God for one's own ends. How do you deal with these temptations? Have you come across people who have played the guru and acted in an authoritarian and unfeeling way?

I find it comforting to know that these temptations exist and constantly threaten me. But I also know that I'm not alone in these temptations; Jesus experienced them too.

29

The Jesus who weeps

In Umberto Eco's novel The Name of the Rose, *there's a bitter dispute over the question whether Jesus laughed. In our society, so focussed on entertainment, that's no longer an issue. We find it more difficult to accept that Jesus wept. We like to imagine a Jesus who was so much himself, was so filled with God, that nothing shook him or upset his equilibrium. But the Gospels tell us of a Jesus who wept: 'As he drew near and came in sight of the city, he wept over it and said, "If only you had recognized on this day what brings you peace. But now it is hidden from your eyes"' (Luke 19.41f.).*

Jesus weeps over the fate of Jerusalem. He foresees that this holy city will be destroyed by the Romans. He has taken great trouble to proclaim the message of the kingdom of God to the people of Jerusalem and to summon them to repentance. But it has been to no avail. His efforts have been in vain. Jerusalem is the fulfilment of all a Jew's dreams. When as a Jew Jesus entered the holy city, his spirits rose. So he is all the more deeply affected when he reflects on the fate of this city. Pagans will destroy the city 'and leave no stone standing on another' (Luke 19.44). Jerusalem was blind and had not recognized that God himself had visited the city in Jesus. That makes Jesus sad, and he weeps over this city. These are tears of sorrow, but also tears of helplessness. He senses that his efforts to convert the city were in vain. He can't get to it, whether through miracles, through words, or through his love.

Another time Jesus weeps over the death of Lazarus. Jesus sees how Mary is weeping for her dead brother and how her friends are also weeping. Then 'he was greatly disturbed and with a profound sigh he said, "Where have you put him?" They said, "Lord, come and see." Jesus wept. The Jews said, "See how he loved him!"' (John 11.33–6). Here we have tears of sorrow for his friend and tears of compassion for the sisters of his dead friend. And the tears are an expression of his love of Lazarus. Jesus shows his feelings. He is utterly human. He undergoes the pain of grief and doesn't get over it through hope for the resurrection of Lazarus. And he feels with the sisters of the dead man. Their sorrow sets off his own. Twice it is said in this scene that Jesus was greatly disturbed and sighed profoundly (verses 33 and 38). The Greek word for indignation used here means that the sorrow is mixed with anger. Despite his close relationship with the Father, Jesus feels pain at the loss of a friend. Mourning always means pain and anger at the same time. Here Jesus feels both. The tears aren't just tears of compassion but also tears of helplessness and anger. Jesus doesn't close himself to the situation. He's wholly involved in it. He's affected by the situation of people and reacts with strong feelings that express his humanity.

For Buddha, contact with the world is the ground of all suffering. So he breaks off contact with the world in order to experience inner freedom in laughter. Jesus allows himself to be touched. He endures the suffering. He feels compassion. He weeps because he is affected in his innermost being. The Jesus who weeps is closer to me than Buddha, who cannot be moved and cannot be touched. Jesus also feels with me. And he encourages me to allow the tears which aren't wept, so that through these tears I come into contact with my heart, in which are love and pain, sorrow and joy. 'If you have a heart, you can be saved,' says Abba Pambo. Jesus had a heart; he invites me to trust my heart and to accept the feelings that are in it.

When was the last time that you wept? What happens when you weep? And what do you feel when you can't weep? Are you afraid that if you allow tears to come, they'll never stop?

Do you let yourself be touched by the suffering of others? Or do you hide your feelings, so that you can seem cool to everyone? The Jesus who weeps invites you to let your tears flow and to trust them. They will lead you through the sorrow to new life.

30

The Jesus who washes feet

At the last meal that they have together before his death, Jesus washes his disciples' feet. At a Jewish party it was customary for a slave to wash the guests' feet. Since at that time people went around barefoot or in sandals, their feet were dirty, so it was sensible to wash them. The washing refreshed not only the feet but the whole person. Since very few people wore sandals at that time, the feet were often injured. The slave who washed feet took them in his hands carefully and inspected them for wounds. Then he anointed the wounds with oil. Oil was a favourite medicament in antiquity. Jesus performs the service of a slave for his disciples. He looks after his disciples' feet.

In the Gospel of John Jesus interprets his washing of the disciples' feet in two ways. The first of these is symbolic. Jesus bows down to people through his incarnation and his death on the cross and washes their feet. Where people have made themselves dirty, where they experience their earthiness day by day in their bodies, Jesus cleanses them by touching them lovingly. Jesus compares his action to a bath: 'No one who has had a bath needs washing, such a person is clean all over' (John 13.10).

So before Jesus washes the disciples' feet they've already had a bath. What kind of a bath was it? For the disciples, the whole of Jesus' activity was a bath. He himself says in the farewell discourses that his words have a cleansing force: 'You are already clean through the word that I have spoken to you' (John 15.3). I've often stumbled over this saying in my meditation. How can I be made clean by a word?

One particular experience made the meaning of this saying clear to me. In the 1970s I often went to hear the celebrated Count Dürckheim. After the third lecture, I knew roughly what he was saying. There was nothing new. But Dürckheim spoke in such a way that after the lecture I felt that I'd been cleansed inwardly. I've listened to speakers who try to persuade their audiences, overwhelming them with a torrent of words. Sometimes I feel that they've made me dirty, swamped me with their unclean emotions. With others the torrent of words is like a bath: I find that I'm at harmony with myself, cleansed.

Jesus evidently spoke to his disciples in such a way that afterwards they felt clean. Their tendency to reject themselves was washed away by the words of Jesus. Their guilt feelings dissolved. They felt cleansed from their guilt. For the disciples, Jesus' activity is like a bath. They've been made clean by his words and the signs that he's done.

Now only their feet needed to be washed for their cleansing to be complete. That happens in the death of Jesus on the cross. There Jesus will cleanse their feet from any dirt. As long as the disciples are still in the world, time and again they will get their feet dirty. If they are to enter the Father's house, they need to have their feet washed. Jesus performs this task for them in his death on the cross.

On the cross Jesus touches people at their most vulnerable point. In Greek mythology that was the Achilles' heel. For even armour doesn't protect a person there. The enemy's arrow can hit him. Death is the wound against which human beings cannot protect themselves. Jesus heals men and women from this deadly wound by coming down to them in his death and carefully taking their Achilles heel into his hands.

The evangelist John understands the death of Jesus on the cross as exaltation. The paradox is that Jesus is exalted and glorified by God at the very point when he bows himself down in the dust of death.

John combined this image of washing feet with another image, that of the snake which Moses hung up on an iron pole in the wilderness. Anyone who looked at the snake raised up on the pole was healed from deadly snake bites. For the Greeks the snake fixed to the pole was a symbol for Asclepius, the god of healing, the patron of all physicians.

Jesus on the cross is the wounded physician. Hanging on the cross he shows us mortal men and women our most vulnerable spot, the wound of death, from which we all suffer and which combines in itself all other wounds. John thinks that a look at Jesus nailed to the cross will heal all our wounds.

The second interpretation of the foot washing that Jesus gives is a moral one: 'I have given you an example, so that you may do as I have done to you' (John 13.15). Jesus is the model for a new kind of behaviour. We are shown to be Jesus' disciples if we wash, not other people's heads, but their feet; if we don't tread on their feet but bow down to touch the injured place and heal it. We show ourselves to be filled by the spirit of Jesus if we act as a bath for others, if we're refreshing, enlivening and cleansing.

You can check the effect that you have on others by the example of Jesus. Are you the kind of person who washes other people's feet or do you tread on them? Are you like a refreshing foot bath, or like someone who overwhelms others with his emotions? How do people feel in your presence?

When you meditate on Jesus' words or his actions, do you then sense how he radiates refreshment, cleansing and life?

What gives you courage to endure your wounds? Are you helped to endure your Achilles' heel by the image of washing feet, because Jesus' hand touches you lovingly?

31

Jesus the son of God

At the hearing before the Sanhedrin Jesus was asked by the elders, high priests and scribes, '"Are you then the son of God?" He answered, "It is you who say I am." Then they cried out, "What other witnesses do we need? We have heard it from his own mouth"' (Luke 22.70f.).

In the Gospel of Matthew, when the high priest hears Jesus' answer he tears his clothes and exclaims in indignation, 'He has blasphemed God' (Matthew 26.65).

Why does the high priest think that what Jesus says is blasphemy? After all, the Bible says that every human being is a son or a daughter of God. But evidently Jesus spoke of himself in a different way, and saw his relationship with God differently. He was condemned because he understood himself as son of God in an unprecedented way.

Many people even today see Jesus as a fascinating man and the founder of a religion. But most of them find it difficult to understand Jesus as son of God. How are we to understand the claim of Jesus of Nazareth to be son of God?

We can approach this statement from two sides, from 'above' and from 'below'. Today people prefer to move upwards from below: I look at the human being Jesus, at the way in which he spoke, at the way in which he encountered people. I look at his freedom, his clarity, his mercy and his love. As I look at the human Jesus, God dawns on me. It isn't just the personality of Jesus that fascinates me. Here I touch on a mystery which transcends the human. It's the mystery of God himself, which shines out on me in the human being Jesus. On the basis of this experience I can say that in this person I encounter God. In it God speaks to me in a unique and absolute way. This man is the son of God.

The early church took the way from above downwards. For centuries it struggled over the right way to understand Jesus as son of God. That was more than mere speculation or pedantry. Whether Jesus is like God or of the same substance as God (*homoi-ousios* or *homo-ousios*) is not unimportant. For it determines how we understand our humanity and how we experience our redemption and transformation. It was important for the early church that the initiative in the incarnation and redemption came from God himself and that everything in us – our alienation, our guilt, our mortality, our hurts, our mortal wound – is transformed and healed by Jesus. The principle was that 'only what is assumed has been saved'. In Jesus God has assumed everything human. He has assumed birth and death, joy and sorrow, darkness and light. So everything has been saved. Only God can save. The Greek church fathers were convinced of that. In his search for fallen humanity God doesn't stop half way, but goes on to where fallen humanity is, in death. And in this the humanity of Jesus is not belittled.

Indeed the mystery of our redemption lies precisely here. In Jesus God didn't assume an ideal, perfect humanity but our humanity with all its strengths and weaknesses, with its abysses and dangers, with its transitoriness and its mortality. Many people think that this Greek way of looking at things is outdated today. But for me a deep experience underlies this understanding of Jesus, the experience that God and human beings belong together inseparably, that God permeates human beings utterly with his love and his divine spirit. The Greek church fathers are responding to our deepest longing when they say how we can succeed in becoming truly human. In our time Heinrich Böll has given a convincing description in his novels of this connection between God becoming human and our becoming truly human. Böll says that the full significance of Jesus first dawned on him when he saw him as son of God, as Jesus Christ: 'The separation of Jesus from the Christ seems to me to be an illegitimate trick which robs the incarnate one of his divinity and in so doing robs all men and women who are still waiting to become truly human. I shall never doubt the presence of the Incarnate One. But Jesus alone? That is too vague, too sentimental for me, too much of a "touching story".'

I've always enjoyed reading Böll's novels. They don't give me an ideal image of Jesus. But in the midst of the human struggle for love to succeed, in the midst of people's loneliness and desperation, sometimes an image of Jesus shines through. It's always a human Jesus who shines out here. But at the same time, for Böll this Jesus is the son of God, the human being in whom God has become human. This is the promise that we too will succeed in becoming truly human.

It's important to me that I'm not alone on the way to becoming human and becoming myself, but am accompanied by someone who is utterly steeped in God. When looking at him I can be confident that all the abysses and inhibitions in me, all that is fragile and all that has failed, will be changed and healed by God and brought together into the unique figure of me which has been sketched by God. Jesus, the word of God made flesh, is for me the promise that God's world will also be made flesh in me. Then I will become wholly human and at the same time God's son.

How do you imagine Jesus as son of God? How do you understand Jesus? For you, is he just a fascinating person, or does God express himself for you in Jesus in a unique and unsurpassable way? Where does the divine in Jesus shine out for you? How do you see God and humanity together in Jesus?

Can you endorse Heinrich Böll's view that your becoming truly human depends on God's becoming human in Jesus? Is it good news for you that Jesus is the son of God who has accepted and redeemed all that is human in you?

How would you formulate the mystery that God has become human in Jesus Christ for yourself? How would you spell it out? What does 'becoming truly human' mean for you?

In prison, the Jesuit priest Alfred Delp, who was murdered by the Nazis, recognized that a person is wholly human only if he or she is seen together with God. Can you confirm that for yourself?

32

The tender Jesus

Heinrich Böll has rediscovered the tenderness of Jesus. In an interview he complained that the church has taken refuge in the arrogance of a dogmatism which knows precisely what is right for everyone and condemns and isolates all those who don't correspond to its norms. Over against that he sets the tenderness of Jesus: 'In the New Testament there is a theology of – I dare to use the word – tenderness, which always has a healing effect: through words, through a laying on of hands that one could also call caressing, through kisses, through shared meals – in my view that is all totally spoiled and perverted by a legalization, one could say by a Romanization, which has turned it into dogmas, principles, catechisms. This element of the New Testament – tenderness – has still to be discovered.'

The tenderness of Jesus becomes evident in his encounter with people, for example with the woman who is a sinner. She washes his feet; he allows her to touch him tenderly and deals tenderly with her himself. Many stories about healings show us the tender Jesus who touches people carefully and tenderly. For me the healing of the deaf and dumb man is an impressive example of this (Mark 7.31–7) A man is brought to Jesus who can't speak, who has been struck dumb, who has fallen silent for fear of not being taken seriously. And he's deaf. He's closed his ears because they can no longer bear the many harsh words of rejection. Jesus takes this terrified and fearful person away from the crowd and pays exclusive attention to him:

> He took him aside to be by themselves, away from the crowd, put his fingers into the man's ears and touched his tongue with

spittle. Then looking up to heaven he sighed; and he said to him, 'Ephphatha,' that is, 'Be opened.' (Mark 7.33).

Jesus gives the deaf and dumb man special treatment. He puts his fingers in the man's ears. The ears are very sensitive. Jesus very tenderly touches these ears, which have heard so many hurtful things. The loving touch is to keep away the hurtful words and once again to open up the ears to words of loving care. With his protective gesture Jesus wants to tell the deaf and dumb man, 'You can hear your longing for relationships even in the harsh and rejecting words of your fellow men and women. Hearing is meant for creating relationships. Listen not only to the words, but also to the heart that can be heard in the voices of others.'

Like Heinrich Böll, we can imagine Jesus' touching of the dumb man's tongue with his spittle as a kiss. Jesus evidently had no fear of such intimate contact in a kiss. With his tongue he loosens the tongue of the dumb man. Then Jesus looks up to heaven. Loving care opens heaven above this imprisoned man. Jesus' tenderness is bound up with the love of the heavenly Father. It brings God's tender love to human beings. Jesus sighs. He feels with the sick man. He has compassion on him. He opens his heart to him. In this sphere of human and divine love Jesus now encourages the deaf and dumb man: '"Ephphatha", that is, "Be opened"' (Mark 7.33). Only if the heavens open over him, and only in the presence of a compassionate heart can the dumb man open his mouth and 'speak clearly'. He can express the feelings and needs that are in him without the fear that his words will be twisted, that he will be branded or condemned for his words. In the sphere of love we can venture to utter words which create relationships and reach the hearts of others.

Jesus is tender with men and women. He touches tenderly the woman who has been going around for eighteen years with a bent back (Luke 13.10–17). He allows himself to be touched by the woman who has been suffering from a flow of blood for twelve years (Mark 5.25–34). The Jews regarded this woman as unclean. No one wanted to come into contact with her. Jesus isn't afraid that touching her will make him unclean. He rewards her courage by healing her. In his tenderness Jesus displays feminine and motherly features, as he also does when healing a blind man: 'He took the blind man by the hand, led him out of the village, smeared his eyes with spittle, laid hands on him and asked him, "Can you see anything?"' (Mark 8.23). Spittle is always tender and motherly. The mother strokes her hurt child with some spittle and says, 'That'll make it better.' In the spittle Jesus gives something of himself, something intimate. When the blind man can see only shadows, Jesus once again puts his hands on his eyes. Through his hands he makes not only God's healing power but also his personal love stream into the other person. Jesus treats the blind man like a mother who touches and caresses her child tenderly. Like a mother he senses that the sick person needs yet more care, yet more tender contact, before he dares to open his eyes wide and see everything as it really is.

In the spiritual tradition some authors describe Jesus as a mother. By this they want to indicate that Jesus is not only as tender as a father but also turns to wounded people in a motherly way and touches them with tender hands. His tenderness is shaped by the particular relationship in which he is involved. Jesus doesn't escape into ideologies or principles, but allows himself to be touched by people and turns to them as his heart tells him, not as the norm prescribes.

Jesus wants to trust me to trust my feelings more than the opinions of those around me or the inner objections which prevent me from turning lovingly towards another person: 'Perhaps he wouldn't like it. What will the others think? Am I showing too much intimacy here? Am I being dictated to by my own needs?' Jesus is in contact with his heart. And so he also senses the hearts of others and does what is right for himself and them.

Are you tender with yourself? Are you afraid of tender contact? What happens in you when someone touches you tenderly? Do you long for tenderness, and how do you deal with your longing?

Can you touch others tenderly? How do you react to the impulse to turn lovingly to someone else? Are you put off by objections like, 'Perhaps he wouldn't like it. What will the others think? Am I showing too much intimacy here? Am I being dictated to by my own needs?' Try today to trust your feelings and show people the intimacy to which your feelings prompt you.

When Heinrich Böll writes about hiding behind norms and principles to avoid the tenderness of Jesus, do you know what he means?

33

Jesus the messiah

When Jesus asks the disciples who they think that he is, Peter replies, 'You are the messiah, the son of the living God!' (Matthew 16.16). Jesus praises Peter for this answer: 'You are blessed, Simon Bar-Jonah; for flesh and blood have not revealed this to you, but my Father in heaven' (Matthew 16.17).

For us today the concept of messiah is a remote one. However, for the Jews of Jesus' time it embodied all their longing for the intervention of God in this world. The messiah would lead the people to freedom and liberate them from foreign rule. He would restore confidence in themselves to the oppressed people. He would lead them into the promised land, a land in which all could be completely themselves, no longer oppressed by any 'overseers' who forced them to work harder and harder. The messiah would make God's rule visible on earth. Then God would be near to all men and women. The fruit of this divine presence would be a peace that could never again be shattered.

However, it isn't enough for me to outline the concept of the Messiah simply in terms of the theology of that time. What does this term mean personally for me today? Is it an image which puts Jesus in a new light for me? Messiah means anointed. When I investigate this image, I'm led to the mystery of oil. People anoint themselves with oil to make themselves attractive. Oil makes one's face shine and has a pleasant fragrance. Those who anoint themselves can smell the fragrance of the oil. Oil gives people the living energy that it has drawn from the sunshine and the earth. Oil refreshes the exhausted, heals the sick, cools fever, soothes pains. Oil smoothes whatever is rough and harsh.

The New Testament translates the Hebrew word messiah into Greek, *Christos*. And so it speaks of Jesus the Christ, Jesus the anointed one. The church fathers do the same. This is how Peter Chrysologus sees things: 'After the son of God had poured himself into our flesh with all the ointment of divinity, he was called Christ because of this oil. And he over whom God has been poured, into whom God has streamed in such a way is the sole author of this name.' During his life Jesus preserved the divine oil in the vessel of his body. In death he broke the vessel and poured out the fragrant oil of the divine love on us all. So with a term taken from the Song of Songs (1.1) the church fathers call Jesus 'outpoured oil'.

These notions of the church fathers echo the experience that through Jesus they felt new born, filled with the fragrance of divine love, strengthened with oil that made their limbs supple, cleansed from the dirt of guilt. For them the concept of Christ was no empty dogmatic concept but an image that fascinated them, since they associated a daily experience with the oil. After bathing they anointed themselves with oil, enjoyed its fragrance and thus physically experienced its beauty and worth.

When in the Gospel of Matthew Peter calls Jesus the messiah, he's thinking not so much of oil as of freedom and peace. Matthew uses the concept of messiah as he has found it in the Moses tradition. For many Jews, Moses was the model of the messiah. He led his people to freedom. For Matthew, Jesus is a second Moses. Like Moses he gives five great speeches and performs ten miracles. By his word Jesus the messiah proclaims God's mercy. By his actions he shows God's liberating activity. By his words and actions Jesus touches people's hearts.

Both the Jewish concept of messiah and the Greek image of Christ the anointed describe Jesus as someone who gives new radiance to our life, who leads us into the land in which we delight in the dignity of our humanity and may enjoy the fragrance of divine love. Today we usually talk about Jesus Christ. Most people don't know what this means. For them 'Christ' is just some kind of proper name. It remains empty, not filled with experience. This name is important to me personally. For me it means that I expect from Jesus a restoration of my divine dignity and beauty. And for me the name also contains the experience of oil and anointing, of the fragrance of oil after a refreshing bath.

How do you feel after a bath? How do you feel about rubbing a pleasant skin oil on you? Try to associate this experience with people you meet. What people can you say give you such joy that you feel anointed by them? What is there about these people? What do they radiate?

Now try to associate this experience with Jesus the Christ, the anointed. Then perhaps it will dawn on you what Christ means. He can refresh you, soothe you, heal you, bring you to life and make you beautiful. Perhaps then you will understand what Ambrose, one of the most poetic church fathers of the fourth-century Roman church, means when he praises the 'new fragrance of the words of Jesus'.

34

Jesus the king

In politics kings have had their day. When we say that someone is a king, we mean that he radiates dignity. But if someone always wants to be king, we develop an antipathy to him. He always wants to have a central position and to dominate everything. For fairy tales and myths the king is always an archetypal image, an image of the whole person, the person who rules himself instead of being ruled by other powers.

In fairy tales there are always three king's sons who go out to seek the water of life. There are three spheres in human beings which have to be transformed if they are to find their true selves. Greek philosophy – like that of Plato – sees the king as the true wise man who knows about ideas. He knows about the heights and depths of life, the mysteries of light and darkness.

The Bible calls Jesus a king only in parables and in the passion story. In the discourse about the judgement of the world Jesus compares himself with the king who says to the sheep, 'Come you blessed of my Father, take as your heritage the kingdom which has been destined for you since the creation of the world' (Matthew 25.34). On the cross above his head 'an inscription was attached indicating the charge against him: "This is Jesus, the king of the Jews"' (Matthew 27.37). The people mocked him as king: 'If you are the king of the Jews, then help yourself' (Luke 23.37). For the Romans the title king is the reason for executing Jesus; for the Jews it's the occasion for mocking him. Jesus doesn't correspond to their image of a king. The cross puts in question their understanding of what a king is. Jesus isn't the king that the Jews expected.

John shows us in his Gospel how Jesus understands himself as king. When interrogating Jesus, Pilate puts to him the clear question, 'Are you the king of the Jews?' (John 18.33). Jesus answered: 'My kingdom is not of this world. If it was of this world, my people would fight so that I was not handed over to the Jews. But my kingdom is not of this world' (John 18.36).

With these words Jesus interprets his kingship in a completely new way. Jesus is a royal personage. But his kingdom isn't of this world. Jesus has his kingly dignity from God. So no one can dispute his kingship. What Jesus says of himself here is a promise for every Christian. I too can say of myself, 'My kingdom is not of this world.' There is a sphere in me over which the world has no power. There is a kingly dignity in me which no one can take from me, my 'inner kingdom'. Where I am completely myself I am invulnerable. For there Christ is in me with his royal power.

The paradox is that it is in his suffering that Jesus speaks of his kingdom. At the very point where Jesus has been condemned, scourged and nailed to the cross, he is king. So despite all the outward humiliation and hurt Jesus strides through his passion in a sovereign way.

That means that the reality of my own inner kingdom also continues on my way of the cross. At the very point where I am judged and condemned by others, where I am misunderstood, where I am scourged, insulted, made to look ridiculous, there is something in me that no one can hurt. Where I fail, there is something in me that cannot be broken. Even in my dying the divine dignity cannot be taken from me. The knowledge of my kingdom which is not of this world continues to work in this world's freedom, as confidence, as calmness and inner strength which no one can break.

When Pilate asks, 'Are you a king, then?' Jesus replies, 'It is you who say that I am a king. I was born for this, I came into the world for this, to bear witness to the truth; and all who are on the side of truth listen to my voice' (John 18.37). Jesus understood his kingship as a testimony to the truth. The Greek image of the king shines out in this saying. Jesus is the king who lifts the veil that lies over reality.

He is the wise man who leads us into the truth, who makes us share in his knowledge.

Knowledge comes from seeing. Jesus sees to the heart of things. He looks at human beings from God's perspective. He knows 'what is in man' (John 2.25). His knowledge of the mystery of human beings comes to a climax on the cross. The cross is an image for the unity of all opposites. On the cross Jesus comes into contact with heaven and earth, with light and darkness, with good and evil, with the conscious and the unconscious, with woman and man. On the cross he is initiated into the mystery of God and humankind. From the cross, John says, he will draw all men and women to him. On the cross he is the king who leads us into the truth, who opens our eyes so that we know the ground of all being: God, who is love.

For me, Jesus the king is an invitation to discover my own royal dignity and to recognize it particularly in my suffering, in my weakness and helplessness, in my being nailed to the cross. Just imagine that in your sickness, in the conflicts of your everyday life, in situations in which you feel weak, sensitive, uncertain, there is something in you which no one can lay hands on because it is divine. If that is the case, how would you go through your everyday life, what would you feel about yourself if your boss criticized you, if something in your life went wrong, if you felt hurt in your partnership or friendship?

35

Jesus the prophet

The people say of Jesus, 'He is a prophet, like one of the prophets of old' (Mark 6.15). In the Gospel of Luke Jesus understands himself as a prophet and therefore deliberately goes to the end of his way in Jerusalem: 'For it cannot be that a prophet perishes outside Jerusalem' (Luke 13.33). Jesus recognizes that his way will lead him to a violent death on the cross. His fate will be that of many prophets. Many prophets emerged in the history of the Jewish people and incorruptibly proclaimed the will of God. Like them, Jesus too must pay for his message of God's healing presence with his death.

In the Gospel of John the Samaritan woman says to Jesus, 'Sir, I see that you are a prophet' (John 4.19). John himself depicts Jesus as the prophet who fulfils the longing of the Jews for a prophet who is like Moses, indeed greater than Moses. This longing was kindled by the book of Deuteronomy. There Moses says of himself, 'The Lord your God will raise up in your midst, from among your brothers, a prophet like me' (Deuteronomy 18.15). After the multiplication of the loaves, the people say, 'This is really that prophet who shall come into the world' (John 6.14). They believe that in Jesus the promise that they have hoped for since the book of Deuteronomy has been fulfilled.

What is a prophet? The Hebrew term for prophet, *nabi*, really means someone whom God has called. The prophet is the one called by God and at the same time the one who calls, who interprets God's will and proclaims it to people. But the Old Testament knows another term for the prophet, 'the seer'. 'For the man who is called prophet used to be called seer' (1 Samuel 9.9). The Greek word *prophetes* means someone who speaks openly and in an authoritative way. A prophet is a person who communicates to others on behalf of someone else, in his place and at his command. In their oracle sanctuaries the Greeks knew of prophets who proclaimed the will of the deity. In Greece the poets understood themselves as prophets of the divine muses and the philosophers understood themselves as prophets of truth.

Jesus is the one who proclaims to us what he has seen. 'The only one, who is God and rests close to the Father's heart, has made him known' (John 1.18). Jesus is the true seer. He makes us share in what he has seen. When he pours out his Spirit on us, we ourselves become prophets. That is what Luke tells us in the Acts of the Apostles: 'I shall pour out my Spirit on all flesh. Your sons and daughters will be prophets, your young men will see visions, your old people will dream dreams' (Acts 2.17, quoting Joel 3.1).

Those who dream see more deeply and more widely. They recognize new possibilities for a future human society. The dream has always been a source of inspiration, fantasy and creativity. Prophets get things moving. They open up new horizons for us. Time and again, prophets in the history of Christianity have had visions and dreams. Martin Luther King had a dream of a new society in which black and white lived together. Pope John XXIII dreamed of a new church which opened its windows wide.

In baptism we are anointed to be prophets. The prophet is an important image for understanding ourselves. For me, being a prophet means expressing something of God through my life that can find expression only in this world. Through me God wants to say something to this world which he can communicate only through me, as the person I have become. Every human being is unique. Each of us is a unique image that God has made for himself, only of this particular person. My task consists in making this unique image of God shine out through me in this world. Jesus, the prophet sent by God, encourages me to trust what I have to say. At the same time he makes me sensitive to the fact that I cannot proclaim anything by myself, but only if I am transparent to God's Spirit.

Think about what God can express in this world only through you. You can get some idea of the unique things that only you can say in this world if you look at your life story, your gifts, but also your hurts, the experience that you've had, the heights and depths of your career. Jesus as the prophet brings out of you what God has put into you. And he gives you the certainty that you're special and unique, that you have something to say to this world. What is the message that only you can proclaim?

36

Jesus the priest

There are priests and priestesses in all religions. They are mediators between God and human beings. They link human beings to God. The Romans called the priest pontifex *('bridge builder'). He has the task of building bridges by which men and women can go to God and God can come to them. Rituals are often such bridges. But so too is pastoral care. In Asian cultures the priest, particularly as a contemplative, is someone who opens up this world for God and thus creates the link between human beings and God. The priest is also the changer and the transformer, who transforms the earthly into the divine. He is the divine tracker who discloses the traces of God in human life. And he is the advocate of men and women before God, the intercessor.*

Jesus never calls himself a priest. However, the Letter to the Hebrews uses the image of the priest to describe the nature of Jesus: 'The principal point of all that we have said is that we have a high priest of exactly this kind. He has taken his seat at the right of the throne of divine Majesty in the heavens, and he is the minister of the sanctuary and of the true tent which the Lord, and not any man, set up' (Hebrews 8.1f.).

The author of the Letter to the Hebrews wants to sketch out a new theology, in order to give courage and confidence to Christians who have grown weary. He uses the image of the high priest to bring Jesus near to the people of his time and to enthuse them about him. In the Old Testament the main task of the high priest is to intercede from the human side and to offer gifts and sacrifices for sins. The author of Hebrews wants to use the image of the high priest to make clear Jesus' solidarity with men and women. Two basic ills of men and women appear in the Letter to the Hebrews: our solitude and our suffering because of our guilt. We feel abandoned to all our distress. Jesus intercedes for us. In him our life even now reaches into the divine sphere, where Jesus sits at the right hand of the Father. Guilt and guilt feelings are as oppressive for many people as they were then, at the end of the first century. When the author speaks of the blood of Jesus which is shed for us, this is no bloodthirsty theology, but a human image of Jesus' solidarity with people who are tortured by guilt feelings. Jesus' blood is a sign of a love which can cleanse us from our guilt and our guilt feelings.

The word 'sacrifice' keeps occurring in the Letter to the Hebrews. We find this term, too, difficult today. In the light of its Hebrew root, 'sacrifice' really means 'approach to God'. In the image of the high priest who alone may enter the Holy of Holies in the temple, the author of the Letter to the Hebrews says that Jesus is close to God and leads us into the healing and loving presence of God. Jesus has entered the heavenly sanctuary as our forerunner and has given us 'a safe and firm anchor for the soul which reaches right through inside the curtain' (Hebrews 6.19). Through Jesus we have already entered the Holy of Holies, the heavenly sanctuary, the holy and healing sphere of God. Our soul is already anchored there. So in us there is something that already reaches into God's holy tent.

Only the holy can heal. People in the time of Jesus were convinced of this. Through Jesus we have free access to God, to the holy tent. There we experience healing and salvation. The Letter to the Hebrews also expresses that with the image of God's sabbath rest: in the heavenly tent, as high priest Jesus celebrates the liturgy of God's eternal sabbath rest. In Jesus our restless heart finds rest. There we already take part in God's sabbath rest, in the consummation. By this term 'consummation' (Greek *teleiosis*) the Letter to the Hebrews means that now already, in the midst of our pilgrimage, on which we are oppressed and hemmed in, we have reached our destination. Even now, where we celebrate the liturgy on our earthly wanderings, we have arrived at eternal rest. That gives us confidence for our way.

The image that the Letter to the Hebrews draws of Jesus is a human and a comforting one. The concept of the priest has nothing strange and alienating about it here. As priest, Jesus has made it possible for us to have free access to God. God is no longer the distant one. He has come near to us in Jesus. What Jesus communicates to us is a healing and liberating presence of God, a presence which raises us up, in which we can breathe. God himself is in our midst. He has become our centre. That is what the Letter to the Hebrews wants to say with the image of the priest as mediator between God and human beings. And Jesus is our advocate. He intercedes with God for us. We aren't alone on our way. We have a high priest who understands us, who feels with us (Hebrew 4.15). He stands at our side. In him God himself stands at our side. He is a God of human beings. That is the message of Jesus which the Letter to the Hebrews sets out to communicate to us in language which at first sight is strange, so that 'with full confidence we may approach the throne of grace' (Hebrews 4.16).

What do you associate with the term priest? What experiences do you connect with priests? Presumably these experiences have influenced whether the image of the priest can open up Jesus to you or whether it does more to hinder your way to him.

The priest is an archetypal image which even today touches on the deepest longings of many men and women. What longings are evoked in you when you hear of priests and priestesses? If you direct these longings to Jesus, what does he mean for you then? What then do you discover in him?

37

The Jesus who leads to life

Luke calls Jesus the one who leads to life, the author of life, in Greek archegos tes zoes. What does he mean by this wonderful title that he gives Jesus? What experience underlies this token of honour? Archegos means author, instigator, founder, leader, ruler. For Luke, Jesus is the one who leads to life. He leads us to life, he introduces us to the art of living. He teaches us what life means. As the one who leads to life, Jesus goes before us on our way.

Jesus tells us in a parable what he means when he says that Jesus leads us to life: 'What woman with ten drachmas would not, if she lost one, light a lamp and sweep out the house and search indefatigably until she found it? And then when she had found it, call together her friends and neighbours, saying to them, 'Rejoice with me; I have found the drachma that I lost' (Luke 15.8f.). Ten is the number of completeness. When the woman loses a drachma, she loses herself, she loses her centre. She still goes on functioning, but with no relation to herself. Jesus depicts for us in this woman the state of many people who've lost sight of themselves. Outwardly they seem to keep going, but they aren't in contact with themselves. Jesus compares his own behaviour to that of the woman who goes looking for her lost drachma. Jesus looks for us himself. He lights the lamp of his love, so that we dare to look at ourselves in the light of this lamp. He sweeps out our house, in which a good deal of rubbish has accumulated. He goes in search of us 'diligently', as it says in the parable, until he finds us. Then he celebrates a feast with us, the feast of becoming whole, of becoming human, the feast of life.

In the Gospel of Luke Jesus shows himself in the most varied ways to be the one who leads to life, the author of life. He leads us to life by seeking what is lost in us and restoring us to wholeness. He gives us life with his words and his attitude to life. Jesus wants to open our eyes to true life, particularly in sayings which initially alienate us. He provokes us, so that we become open to authentic life. He opens our eyes so that we discover everything in ourselves that we haven't lived out. Often life drags us along; we haven't really got hold of it. Jesus urges us to have lives of our own. He encourages us to go our own ways. Only by doing that will we come alive, bear witness to life.

Unfortunately many Christians don't understand Jesus as one who leads to life but rather as a refuge from life. Because they're afraid of life and its controversies, they escape to Jesus. But that is to falsify Jesus and his concerns. Jesus is where life is, not where for fear of life we escape into pious rules. Jesus urges us to dare to live our own lives without constantly paying heed to the opinions of others.

What leads you to life? Where do you experience liveliness? What do you long for when you think of life and quality of life? What do you imagine by life?

Who do you allow to urge you to live? Do you find that Jesus is the one who leads you to life? Or do other people, other things, do that? What dawns on you when you look at Jesus as the one who leads to life?

38

Jesus the teacher

Matthew saw Jesus above all as the teacher. He brought together the sayings of Jesus in five long discourses and shaped these artistically. These five discourses correspond to the five books of Moses. So Jesus gives us a new teaching.

For his greatest and probably best-known discourse, the Sermon on the Mount (Matthew 5.1–7.29), like Moses Jesus climbs a mountain: 'He sat down, and his disciples came to him. Then he began to speak and taught them' (Matthew 5.1f.). The Jewish rabbis used to sit down when they were teaching. Sitting is a sign that someone is at rest. The Jews spoke of the chair of teaching, Moses' chair, on which the rabbis sat. But Jesus accuses them of not doing what they teach and of closing the kingdom of heaven to people with their exposition of the law (Matthew 23.13). When Jesus teaches sitting down, he shows that he is sitting on God's chair, that he has his foundation in God and teaches with divine authority. That's what his hearers experience on hearing his first long discourse: 'When Jesus had ended these words the crowd were astounded by his teaching; for he taught as one who has (divine) authority, and not like their scribes' (Matthew 7.28f.).

Jesus begins his teaching with the Beatitudes: 'Blessed are the poor in spirit, for theirs is the kingdom of heaven. Blessed are those who mourn, for they shall be comforted' (Matthew 5.3f.). This introduction alone shows that Jesus is quite a different kind of teacher. He doesn't begin by proclaiming commandments and prohibitions. He doesn't set out a new dogmatic theology, a system of doctrines about God and human beings, but promises people God's salvation. He raises them up with his teaching. He encourages them. He speaks to their heart.

They're moved, touched. When they listen to Jesus they feel uplifted, liberated, accepted. They sense their worth. And in the sayings of Jesus they experience God as a God who wants their salvation, who promises them comfort and hope. God isn't primarily a God who demands, but a God who gives. He gives people a new way to life, a way which can heal the rift that runs through human society. The basic condition of all teaching is that we should know who we are. In the Sermon on the Mount Jesus tells us that we are sons and daughters of God.

The Sermon on the Mount is the exposition of the Lord's Prayer. The Lord's Prayer stands right in the middle of the Sermon on the Mount. And the individual teachings expound what we pray. Jesus shows us the behaviour of those who in prayer experience God as their Father.

The Beatitudes correspond to the petition 'Hallowed be thy name'. God's name is hallowed, God is made manifest in his holiness, when human beings become healthy and whole, when they experience happiness. The petition 'Thy kingdom come' is expounded in the saying about the salt of the earth and the light of the world (Matthew 5.13–16). The kingdom of God becomes visible on earth through the new behaviour of the disciples. In the six antitheses (Matthew 5.21–48) Jesus expounds the will of God as it was really intended. Where the disciples demonstrate this new form of behaviour, God's will is being done not only in heaven but also on earth. The petition about daily bread is then expounded with reference to fasting, almsgiving, prayer, and the call not to be anxious but to trust in God's gracious hand (Matthew 6.1–34). The petition for the forgiveness of sins has its parallel in Jesus' admonition, 'Do not judge, so that you are not judged' (Matthew 7.1). And the petition for God not to lead us into temptation but to deliver us from evil is spelt out in a reference to the false prophets who confuse us (Matthew 7.15–23). Temptation isn't really a matter of being overwhelmed by our errors and weaknesses but rather a confusion in which we no longer know what we're doing, in which our thoughts and feelings are all mixed up and we fall away from God.

If we understand the great discourse of the Sermon on the Mount as an exposition of the Lord's Prayer, we shall recognize how Jesus understood his teaching in principle. He doesn't present teaching consisting of commandments that we have to fulfil. Nor is his teaching something that we can take or leave, with no consequences for our behaviour. The new teaching is also meant to lead to a new way of behaving. But it presupposes a new experience, the experience that we are sons and daughters of God. Praying the Lord's Prayer is to lead us to this new experience.

Prayer transforms the presuppositions of our action. It's also the place where we experience Christ as our true teacher. For Augustine this insight led to the idea of Jesus as the teacher within. When something dawns on us, this insight is conveyed not by the teacher speaking from outside but by Christ, the teacher within: 'We enquire of that teacher to whom the word of scripture refers, according to which Christ dwells in the innermost person (Ephesians 3.17) as God's unchangeable power and eternal wisdom' (Augustine, *De magistro* 11.38). Against the background of this saying of Augustine the theologian Eugen Biser wrote a book entitled *The Inner Teacher*. Jesus is within us. Jesus' teaching isn't a doctrinal system, the letters of which we can argue over. The teacher within wants neither correctness nor dogmatism but a readiness to listen to our inner impulses. There, in our heart, Jesus dwells as our teacher. Jesus as our inner teacher makes us share in what he has experienced, sensed, what he knows. He opens our eyes to see what he has seen.

Are you in contact with your teacher within? Do you listen to the inner voice that shows you the way? What does Jesus, your inner teacher, want to teach you? What new insights do you have about yourself and life, about God and other people, when you contemplate Jesus as teacher?

Read the Sermon on the Mount again and meditate on Jesus' words. Do you agree with Helmut Schmidt's remark that the Sermon on the Mount is useless in politics? If you see the Sermon on the Mount as teaching that arises out of the experience of prayer, how then do you deal with it? Let it attract you to new modes of behaviour, to creativity in dealing with yourself and your fellow men and women.

39

Jesus the story-teller

More than any other teacher before him, Jesus developed his teaching above all in parables. Matthew and Luke have handed on to us many of these parables, which Jesus told to his disciples or even to the crowd. In them Jesus proves to be a brilliant story-teller. Evidently he could talk about human life in such a way that those who heard him fell under his spell. The parables show Jesus as a human being and a story-teller. In them Jesus paints an authentic portrait of himself, and he opens our eyes to the mystery of God and human beings.

In the parables Jesus tells us simply about human life, about people working in the fields, about their experiences in sowing, about how crops grow on the land, about rain and sun. He takes examples from his surroundings, like that of a steward whom his master has dismissed for corrupt practices. Or he gives the example of the owner of a vineyard who hires new labourers at all times of the day. Jesus' stories are so exciting that people pay attention to them. He casts his spell on people. They go along with him. He confirms what they think. Then all at once his story-telling changes. For the conclusion isn't necessarily what people expected.

Jesus opens up everyday experiences to God. He tells of life in such a way that all at once the mystery of God dawns on people. Jesus bewitches his audience with his parables. He transforms their mood into approval of God's action. People feel that Jesus is talking about them and their lives. And all at once he opens their eyes so that they see more deeply, so that they discover God in their lives. For Jesus, God isn't abstract. God becomes visible; he can be experienced in the stories. The art of Jesus is that he doesn't constantly utter the word God and proclaim every possible doctrine about God. Rather, he talks to people in such a way that God dawns on them. When Jesus tells stories, his hearers are as it were created anew. They find that they're transformed by God's grace. When Jesus tells people parables, they're renewed and rescued from patterns of life that bring death.

Among the evangelists, the greatest story-teller is probably Luke the Greek. He described the life of Jesus in a language that enthused his Greek readers. And he shaped the parables of Jesus in such a way that his readers were moved by Jesus' skill in story-telling. In the so-called special parables, which occur only in Luke, the style he uses is that of the inner monologue. The rich man who has had a good harvest says to himself, '"What am I to do? I haven't enough room to store my crops." Then he said, "This is what I will do: I will pull down my barns and build bigger ones, and store all my grain and my goods in them, and I will say to my soul, My soul, you have plenty of good things laid by for many years to come. Take things easy, eat, drink, have a good time"' (Luke 12.17–19). With the aid of the inner monologue Jesus establishes a relationship with the reader. Readers can identify with the words of the story-teller and feel that their own thoughts are being expressed. Luke believes that in this way he is giving an authentic image of Jesus' skill in story-telling. Evidently in his story-telling Jesus had mastered the art of discovering the thoughts of his audience and presenting them in such a way that his hearers felt, 'He's talking about me. He's expressing what I think but never dared to say.' Jesus expresses the thoughts of his hearers and directs them back to God. By his story-telling he opens up the hearts of his hearers to God. Story-telling is a kind of theology which is friendly to men and women. Jesus doesn't lecture. He doesn't force his view of God on people. He doesn't hammer it into them. He tells about their life, so that imperceptibly they rediscover themselves in his stories and open themselves to God in freedom.

What story from the Gospels fascinates you most? What dawns on you when you read this story? What parable offends you? Where a parable offends you, it may point you to a deeper perspective. What fixed view of things does the parable disclose to you? What image of God and of yourself does the parable want to teach you?

How do you feel when you read a parable (the parable of the prodigal son or the ten virgins, the parable of the unjust steward or the godless judge)? Do you perhaps feel reborn or transformed, enchanted or redeemed?

40

The Jesus who prays

The evangelist Luke has also depicted Jesus as a person who prays. Jesus keeps withdrawing into solitude to pray to the Father. Unfortunately Luke doesn't tell us how Jesus prays. Presumably he was simply silent before God and with God. In prayer Jesus was aware of his unity with the Father. Perhaps he held out to the Father all that he had experienced from others.

In prayer Jesus certainly came into contact with his true self and his mission. Prayer gave him the strength to face his task. It gave him the clarity to be able to speak rightly about God and not to be dominated by the emotions of the disciples and the crowd. For him, being alone with his Father was a source from which he could drink.

On many occasions Luke describes how Jesus prays. And he describes in images the effect that his prayer had. Jesus prays at his baptism, which represents the beginning of his public activity. While he is praying, heaven opens above him. For Jesus, prayer is the experience of heaven opening, of always being in contact with his Father when living here on earth, and on the basis of this relationship also being able to open heaven to others. Jesus prays before he calls his disciples. In prayer he recognizes the mystery of human beings; he senses what is good for them and what awakens life in them. Jesus also prays to the Father on the Mount of Transfiguration. His face becomes bright and shining. Everything in him becomes clear, transparent to God's beauty and light. In prayer Jesus comes into contact with his divine quality. His true being appears, and his authentic self also becomes visible to his disciples.

However, for Jesus prayer is not only becoming one with God but also struggling with God. That becomes clear in the garden of Gethsemane. There Jesus kneels before his Father and prays, 'Father, if you are willing, take this cup from me. Yet not my will but yours be done' (Luke 22.42).

Even Jesus didn't find it utterly natural immediately to yield to God's will. He fought with his Father. He struggled for his life. For Jesus, too, was someone who clung to his life. He sensed the inner resistance of his human nature to the way that lay before him. He needed an angel to strengthen him. And then the struggle really started. 'In his anguish he prayed even more earnestly, and his sweat fell to the ground like great drops of blood' (Luke 22.44).

Jesus attempted to overcome his fear in prayer. He was afraid, as we are. But he faced this fear. The Letter to the Hebrews describes Jesus' struggle in prayer in Gethsemane like this:

> During his life on earth, he offered up prayer and entreaty, with loud cries and with tears, to the one who had the power to save him from death, and, winning a hearing by his reverence, he learned obedience, Son though he was, through his sufferings (Hebrews 5.7f.).

In prayer Jesus learned who God was and what God required of him. And in prayer he learned to put himself at God's disposal, to yield to God's will. In prayer he learned obedience, to listen to God's will, and to be ready to obey this will. In prayer Jesus found the strength to go his way to his passion, without becoming bitter or hard.

Jesus' prayer comes to a climax on the cross. 'But Jesus prayed, "Father, forgive them, for they know not what they do"' (Luke 23.34). On the cross he prays for his murderers. In praying for those who have nailed him to the cross he escapes their power. In prayer he turns to the Father, in whom he has the ground of his being. Because he knows that he is so close to his Father, he can pray for his enemies as he dies, so that his murderers cannot destroy the love that fills him. And Jesus' last breath is a prayer, 'Father, into your hands I commend my spirit' (Luke 23.46). Jesus prays the psalm which pious Jews were praying as an evening prayer at that same hour. But he adds the word 'Abba' ('Dear Father'). He still dares to call God his loving Father as he dies. As Jesus prays, he lets himself fall into the loving arms of his Father. Even in death, he cannot fall out of the security that prayer has given him all his life.

What happens when you pray? Do you get the impression that you're praying into a void? Or do you have a sense that God, your Father, your Mother, hears you? Do you find support and security in prayer?

Have you ever experienced the heavens opening above you as you pray, everything being transformed in you, so that you achieve utter clarity?

When praying, have you ever struggled with God – when your best friend was sick or you just couldn't cope? Has prayer changed your fear and your desperation? Or hasn't it changed anything in you and around you?

Even as he was dying Jesus continued to pray for his enemies. Who do you want to pray for today? How could praying change your relationship with those for whom you pray?

41

Jesus the clown

'They dressed him up in purple, twisted some thorns into a crown and put it on him. And they began saluting him, "Hail, king of the Jews!" They struck his head with a reed and spat on him' (Mark 15.17–19). Jesus is mocked as a fool by the soldiers who are preparing for his crucifixion. They do what they want with him. They make him a laughing-stock. They vent their frustration on him. He becomes their plaything.

The earliest depiction of the crucified Jesus that we have is a caricature. Jesus on the cross is depicted with an ass's head. The Romans of the time wanted to mock Jesus, as Pilate's soldiers mocked him, and depict him as a ridiculous figure. Modern literature is fond of portraying Jesus as a fool and a clown. The soldiers treated Jesus as a figure of fun. But modern literature turns the mockery on its head. The one who is mocked becomes a mirror of ourselves. He unmasks us and presents us with the truth about ourselves.

Gerhard Hauptmann wrote a novel entitled *The Fool in Christo*. In Dostoievsky's novel *The Idiot*, Prince Myshkin is an image of Jesus. He suffers from epilepsy. He embodies the pure and altruistic love of Jesus. In a world in which love is mixed up with possessiveness, greed and often enough violence, Dostoievsky can depict Jesus and his divine love only in the figure of a sick fool. In his play *The Anabaptist* Friedrich Dürrenmatt embodied Jesus in the two figures of Jan Matthisson and Knipperdollinck. Jan Matthisson becomes a fool by confronting the bishop's army unarmed. Knipperdollinck, rich man and former burgomaster that he is, becomes a fool by taking seriously the saying of Jesus, 'Sell all you have and give to the poor.' Like Jesus, both die a violent death. In this world of power they have no chance. Yet they continue to protest against this unjust world in which the powerful call the tune, and in so doing unsettle the powerful.

Another image of Jesus which has become fashionable since Harvey Cox's book *The Feast of Fools* is the image of the clown. In German literature it is above all Heinrich Böll who in his novel *The Clown* interprets the main character Hans Schnier in terms of Jesus. Hans Schnier ends up dressed as a clown on the steps of the railway station in Bonn, where he gently intones the song of 'Poor Pope John' on the guitar. Under the mask of a clown, what Jesus of Nazareth means for people shines out.

Jesus may have seemed like a clown to some pious and earnest Pharisees. He provoked the powerful. He unmasked the pious and showed them their shadow side. He set himself above the laws and demonstrated to those who were infuriated at this that in their hearts they were really lawless. When the Pharisees bring him a woman who has been caught in adultery, he unmasks them and their lofty moralistic claims. Instead of discussing law and justice, he bends over and writes with his finger on the ground. He touches the *humus* and has a sense of humour. He plays on the ground like a child and so unmasks the solemnity of the Pharisees (John 8.2–11). Precisely by disarming people like a clown, Jesus shows them up, discloses to them what they're really thinking and what they're longing for. He uncovers their godlessness.

Jesus didn't observe norms. In the eyes of the pious establishment he acted like a fool. In this role he proclaimed a God who wants life, before whom one doesn't need to appear with a serious face, but whom one can encounter in the joyfulness and freedom of the child, the clown and the fool.

Where do you hide behind a solemn and earnest face, the appearance of a knowledgeable and important person? What's disclosed in you when you put aside these masks? Do you recognize in yourself the indignation of the moralist? What lies behind this indignation?

What biblical passages can you think of which portray Jesus as a fool and a clown?

How do you see yourself when you let Jesus take off your masks? What are the masks which most distort your truth?

In Germany at carnival time we deliberately put on masks. We try on other masks to discover our potential. What happens to you when you put on a mask? What do you come into contact with then?

42

The Jesus who experiences suffering

Many people are troubled by the fact that Jesus ends on the cross. So they can't bear to see the cross in schools, in their houses, on the tops of hills and at crossroads. In particular many people who seek their salvation in Eastern or esoteric religions don't find Jesus very sympathetic, because he reminds them of suffering. Time and again I encounter people who turn away from Jesus because he speaks to them too much of suffering. They prefer healing symbols which do them good. They think that the cross glorifies suffering and isn't good for people. It drags them down and makes them aggressive.

I know many people who've been hurt by a false understanding of suffering. In some Christian circles there's a masochistic view of suffering. Suffering is glorified. They don't fight against suffering, but immediately make it into an ideology. One has to accept the suffering and endure it. It brings us nearer to God.

The glorification of suffering has hurt many people. But it's just as hurtful when the suffering is suppressed. For then all those who are hit by suffering feel outsiders. It used to be said, wrongly, that suffering was a punishment from God. However, the present-day view is just as cruel: sufferers have to be kept away from society. They're excluded from the 'club' of the healthy and pushed to the margins. This insulting forgetfulness of suffering is expressed in the verdict of a German court that to accommodate handicapped people in a bed and breakfast place was asking too much of other guests.

Carl Gustav Jung, the Swiss psychotherapist, compared the attitudes of Buddha and Christ to suffering. For Jung, Jesus as a sufferer is more human and more real than Buddha. Jung remarked in his memoirs that Buddha denied himself suffering and therefore also denied himself joy. He was cut off from feelings and emotions and therefore wasn't really human. In a conversation with a Protestant theologian Jung told of his visit to India. There, he said, it had dawned on him that the attitude to suffering was a fundamental question which determined whether people became truly human. The West attempted to suppress suffering by covering it up with drugs. The East attempted to dissolve suffering by giving up contact with the world. For Buddha the cause of suffering was contact with the world. But the real way was to go through the suffering. Suffering has to be overcome, and can be overcome only by enduring it. Here Jung pointed to the cross that hung in his study. He thought that we could learn to cope rightly with suffering only through the crucified Jesus.

Jesus had experience of suffering. He didn't evade people's suffering but faced their sicknesses and needs. Nor did he flee from his own suffering, though he didn't seek it either. He was hurt when people rejected him, when the Sadducees engineered his execution, when Judas betrayed him and the disciples forsook him. At those times he endured all those things that cause human suffering: loneliness, forsakenness, condemnation, repudiation, hurt, insult, mockery, being stripped naked, being made to look ridiculous, being nailed down, being crucified.

Jesus' death was the culmination of his suffering. There he hung on the cross, gaped at and mocked by his enemies, forsaken by his friends. Indeed some theologians think that his cry 'My God, my God, why have you forsaken me?' points to an experience of godforsakenness. At least on the cross Jesus had to struggle to hold on to God, who had not preserved him from death.

Jesus' experience of suffering was a comfort and an encouragement to the early Christians. It prevented them from repressing their suffering. It gave them the strength to endure their suffering in a hostile environment. Jesus as the one who had experienced suffering didn't lead the early Christians astray into masochistic behaviour. On the contrary, he strengthened them so that they could stand up for themselves and their faith, even when they were attacked by outsiders. They didn't avoid suffering by resorting to self-pity, but as disciples of Jesus took upon themselves everything that went against their view of life. As they contemplated the suffering Jesus they could keep their dignity as human beings, even if the hostile environment wanted to rob them of it.

Nowadays there are inhuman theories about suffering: every individual is to blame for his or her suffering. We all create our own suffering. Such an attitude means that suffering is always also bound up with guilt feelings and self-reproaches. Of course there is suffering that I bring down on myself. But there's also suffering that just hits me. When I read about the passion of Jesus and steep myself in it, I stop asking who is to blame for my suffering, whether I've caused it myself or whether someone else or even God has brought it upon me. Then I try to do everything in my power to remove suffering from the world. But if I can't change it, I accept it. I then know that I'm not left alone in my suffering. I experience fellowship with Jesus. This experience of fellowship with Jesus has already made it possible for many people to maintain their dignity in suffering, humiliation and oppression. I'm helped by contemplating the suffering Jesus to say yes to whatever afflicts me. Then the suffering doesn't make me bitter, but opens me up to my true self, which at the level of the soul is intact from all sickness and distress. It becomes a place where I have some idea of what the mystery of my life is. And it becomes a place where God dawns on me in a new way as the one who holds me in his good hand, even in suffering.

How far do you evade suffering, the suffering of your fellow men and women and your own suffering? How do you deal with people who have experienced suffering, who are mourning the loss of a loved one? Can you put yourself in their place?

Jung says that those who evade the suffering that is essentially bound up with being truly human look for substitute sufferings. For him these are neuroses.

Do you look for substitute suffering in order to avoid real suffering? What happens when you suppress suffering? Does it make you happier? Or are you haunted by the fear that it could also happen to you? How do you cope with your fear?

How do you cope with the suffering that hits you? How far is Jesus an encouragement to you to accept your life as it is?

43

The solitary Jesus

'Life is solitude. No one knows anyone else. Everyone is alone.' This remark by Hermann Hesse expresses how many people feel about life. Despite all the networking, despite ever new means of communication, many people feel lonely. They have lots of contacts, but no real relationships. They isolate themselves in great apartment blocks. They're lonely in the midst of the crowd.

Jesus was constantly surrounded by people. They had great expectations of him. They pressed in on him; they wanted him to lay hands on them and heal them. The Gospels report the constant throng that Jesus had to endure. Nevertheless Jesus was also solitary. He kept withdrawing into solitude. He used solitude to come into contact with himself and his source. In solitude he experienced the company of his heavenly Father.

Jesus was solitary in the midst of people. That emerges from a remark made by John: 'But Jesus knew all people and did not trust himself to them; he never needed evidence about anyone; he could tell what someone had within' (John 2.24).

Jesus encounters everyone with great openness. But there was also something in him that he didn't yield to others, that he kept for himself. For all the intimacy, a distance remained. Certainly he had friends, men and women, like Lazarus, Mary and Martha. But in the depths of his soul some loneliness remained, a sense of being misunderstood.

Jesus was different from other people. He couldn't explain himself to his disciples. They kept getting him wrong. They didn't understand what he meant. When he came down from the Mount of Transfiguration he met his disciples, who had proved incapable of healing a boy who was possessed. Instead of paying attention to the boy, they were arguing with the crowd. Then came an outburst from Jesus: 'Faithless generation, how much longer must I be among you? How much longer must I put up with you?' (Mark 9.19). It wasn't easy for Jesus to feel lonely, to feel that even his followers didn't understand him.

Peter, whom Jesus had chosen to be the rock of his church, objected when Jesus spoke of his imminent suffering. Jesus rebuked him sharply: 'Get behind me, Satan. You are thinking not as God thinks, but as human beings do' (Mark 8.33). Jesus has to go his way of suffering alone, without the comfort and fellowship of his disciples.

When Jesus feels lonely on the Mount of Olives and needs the company of his disciples, the disciples take refuge in sleep. Disappointed, he says to Peter, 'Simon, are you sleeping? Could you not watch with me one hour?' (Mark 14.37). Jesus struggles with God in prayer. When he returns to the disciples, despite his admonition they've fallen asleep again. When he is arrested, 'all forsook him and fled' (Mark 14.50). Peter observes events from afar. But when a servant girl and later other bystanders ask him three times about Jesus, each time Peter denies Jesus. He swears, 'I do not know this man of whom you speak' (Mark 14.71). Jesus dies on the cross, forsaken by his disciples. Only some women who had accompanied him looked on from afar (Mark 15.40f.).

In the Gospel of John it becomes clear that Jesus can accept and endure his loneliness because he knows that he is one with his Father in heaven. 'The time will come – indeed it has come already – when you will be scattered, each going his own way and leaving me alone. Yet I am not alone, because the Father is with me' (John 16.32). People forsake him. Even his disciples withdraw, each to his home. Everyone is self-centred. They all simply want to save their own skins. But precisely in this loneliness, when he is forsaken by his friends, Jesus doesn't feel alone. For his Father is with him. That transforms his loneliness. It becomes a oneness that he has with the Father and the Father has with him.

Jesus isn't the successful man but the solitary, who can't communicate to others much of what moves him. That's a comfort to me in my solitude. I may face my solitude. Solitude isn't just a deep experience of the presence of God, the blissful experience of being one with God. Solitude can also be painful. I feel misunderstood, abandoned. No one supports me when things get serious. No one stands by me when I fail. They all know better. They leave me out in the cold. For me Jesus is the one who supports me through all the stages of my loneliness. In his presence I sometimes no longer feel lonely. In my relationship with him I dare to acknowledge some of my loneliness, to face up to it and endure it.

When do you feel lonely? Have you ever felt forsaken? Does fear of being forsaken keep welling up in you? How do you deal with your loneliness? Do you flee from it or do you endure it? Does the image of the lonely Jesus help you to face your loneliness?

Like Jesus, Dag Hammarskjöld, the UN Secretary General who influenced the fate of the world almost more than anyone else, experienced deep loneliness. But in faith he found a way of dealing with his loneliness. He summed up his way like this: 'Pray that your loneliness may spur you on to find something which you can live for, which is big enough to die for.' Perhaps this remark will help you to deal creatively with your loneliness.

44

The crucified Jesus

The disciples had hoped that Jesus 'would be the one who would redeem Israel' (Luke 24.21). But the Romans nailed this Jesus to the cross. Crucifixion was the cruellest of punishments, one that the Romans used on rebels and criminals. It was a pitiless death: those who hung on the cross gradually became unable to breathe and had to die under the gaze of the onlookers. For the disciples the crucifixion of Jesus was a bitter disappointment. Their hope in the messiah had been shattered. They had to cope with this shock. Their first reaction was flight, and this is described in the story of the disciples on the Emmaus road.

Over the course of time the first Christians reflected on why Jesus died on the cross. They looked in holy scripture to discover what saving meaning could lie in his crucifixion. Paul grappled most intensively with this fact of the crucifixion of God's anointed. For him the cross became the image of his redeemed and liberated existence. The cross showed him that the standards of the world have been done away with. The cross showed another world: the world of grace. Our achievements are unimportant. The cross of Jesus has 'crossed out' all our efforts to make ourselves righteous by our own efforts and by our own standards. From now on all that matters is God's unconditional love, which embraces all that is abysmal and unrighteous in us. Thus for Paul the cross becomes an image of grace and freedom from all pressure to achieve and from the desire to put on a good appearance for other people.

The cross has a different significance for each of the evangelists. For Matthew it symbolizes the powerlessness of Jesus. Jesus is the merciful prophet who is not concerned with power, who allows himself to be arrested and killed without offering violence. For Mark the cross becomes the victory of Jesus over the powers of darkness. In Luke the cross is the expression of tribulations which we too must endure on our way to God's glory. John probably penetrated most deeply into the interpretation of the cross. For him Jesus showed his love to the end on the cross. He has initiated us into the mystery of the love of God who gave us his son that we might have life in him. So the early Christians marked themselves with the sign of the cross. They so to speak inscribed on their bodies the love of God which has shone out most clearly in the cross of Jesus. The cross is at the same time the symbol of all the oppositions of this world. So it indicated to the first Christians that everything in them rested in God's love and was healed; that there was nothing in them that wasn't transformed by the love of Jesus.

However, in every interpretation of the cross there remains the offence that it causes. This is the scandal that Jesus, the messiah, God's son, for whom the nations waited, was nailed to the cross by his fellow men and there died a cruel death. For many Christians the cross represents a great challenge to their image of God. Often enough, people have associated the cross with an aggressive and callous image of God. Some people think that God required the death of his son as expiation for our sins. But the Bible never says this. On the cross Jesus reveals to us the God who suffers with us, who enters into our pain and endures it to the end, thus transforming it.

The cross prompts two kinds of feeling in me. The first is incomprehension. How could God allow Jesus to come to such a cruel end on the cross? Although I know that it was human beings who nailed Jesus to the cross, there remains the provocation, the harshness and incomprehensible nature of this death. It raises questions about my image of God and my image of Jesus. The other feeling is one of being filled with love. When I look at Jesus hanging on the cross with outstretched arms and dying there, I feel that I'm loved uncon-ditionally. In the depth of my heart I know that in the end Jesus also died for me. He held nothing back. On the cross he gave everything, he opened himself for me. His outstretched arms are an invitation to me to feel secure in his love. When I kneel before the cross all self-accusations cease, and my heart becomes still. I know that all is well. Everything is embraced by his love.

What do you associate with the cross? Do you have a cross in your home? What does it remind you of? What does the cross symbolize for you? Is it a sign of salvation that gives you inner peace, a sign of hope, a sign of faith, or does it provoke aggression in you?

The Syrian church knew a marvellous formula for the sign of the cross. When you make the sign of the cross, from the forehead to the stomach, from the left shoulder to the right, you can say: 'In the name of the Father who devised me and created me. In the name of the Son who descended into my humanity. And of the Holy Spirit, who turns the left into the right.' The left can be the unconscious, the unsuccessful, unhappiness. But it can also symbolize the side of the heart, the feelings, love, creativity. In his cross Christ made the unconscious conscious, changed unhappiness into happiness, transformed failure. And he associated the heart with action. He let the love of the heart, the left side, flow into the right side of conscious action. If you make the sign of the cross very carefully, you can sense the tenderness in this gesture. Everything in you is touched with God's love: thought, vitality and sexuality, the conscious and the unconscious, the male and the female.

45

The risen Jesus

The experience which transformed the fearful and terrified disciples into bold witnesses to Jesus was the resurrection of Jesus. We can no longer say precisely what this experience of the resurrection was. It wasn't a figment of the imagination but an experience which moved the disciples deeply and completely transformed them. Jesus the risen one appeared to them. They saw him. They met him. Their meeting with the risen Jesus opened their eyes to who he really was. They knew that the Jesus who had gone with them through Galilee and Judaea is alive. He didn't remain in death. Now he lives in God's glory. He sits at God's right hand. God has made the one whom human beings nailed to the cross Lord of the whole world. This is the revaluation of all values. And it gives us hope that for us, too, all distress and destruction can be transformed, that our life too will ultimately bear fruit and in death will issue in the glory of God.

The disciples' encounter with the risen Christ completely turned their thinking upside down. They couldn't understand what had happened. So they attempted to interpret what God has done in the crucified Jesus in terms of the Bible. Luke uses Psalm 16 to explain Jesus' resurrection; he understands it as a promise for Jesus: 'You will not abandon me to the underworld, or allow your holy one to see corruption' (Acts 2.27).

Psalm 16 describes the close fellowship between pious people and God. The pious person doesn't lose sight of God. 'I have the Lord before my eyes constantly. He stands at my right hand and nothing can shake me' (Psalm 16.8; Acts 2.25). He trusts that his inner fellowship with God cannot be broken even by death. As son of God and as God's anointed, Jesus' association with God is so close that this fellowship cannot be broken by death. The resurrection of Jesus makes us, too, hope that in death we cannot fall out of fellowship with God. Jesus has proclaimed to us that God loves us unconditionally. As God's beloved we will not remain in death. Death has no more power over us. It is merely the gateway to eternal fellowship with God. For the disciples, the resurrection is also the assurance that love is stronger than death. The love with which God loves us cannot be destroyed even by death.

Luke doesn't interpret the resurrection of Jesus only through the sermons that he puts in the mouths of Peter and Paul; he also tells us a number of stories about how Jesus' disciples encountered him. In these stories it becomes clear how we can encounter the risen Christ. For Luke, resurrection isn't an event that one should discuss. Rather, resurrection always takes place where Jesus encounters the disciples as the risen Christ. Luke depicts this in the wonderful story of the disciples on the road to Emmaus (Luke 24.13–35). Two disciples are fleeing in disappointment from Jerusalem, the place of their hope. They talk together about their disappointment. While they are deep in conversation Jesus meets them, coming towards them. But they don't recognize him. Only when he has explained to them from scripture the events that they've experienced and then joins them for a meal do they recognize him. But as soon as they recognize him he becomes invisible and disappears from their sight. Like the disciples on the Emmaus road, we too often run away from the disappointments of our lives. Luke wants to encourage us by showing that resurrection can happen on the way as long as we still keep talking about our shattered illusions. Then all at once we will understand the meaning of all that has happened to us. Our eyes will be opened. We will know that we aren't alone. The risen Christ goes with us on our way. He breaks the bread for us. But we can't hold on to the experience of the risen Christ. As soon as we recognize him, he escapes from our sight and our grasp.

John tells us another resurrection story. It shows us that the risen

Christ encounters us in the futility of our everyday life (John 21.1–14). The disciples have been working in vain all night. They haven't caught a single fish. When they row to the shore, disappointed, they see a man standing on the bank. He speaks to them lovingly and tells them to go out once more and cast the net on the right side. 'They cast the net and could not get it in again because it was so full of fish' (John 21.6). Then the beloved disciples recognize who this man on the shore is: 'It is the Lord' (John 21.7). The risen Christ turns the night of futility into a morning of life and love.

'It is the Lord.' That for me is the experience of the resurrection. When I say this sentence to myself in the middle of my work, in discussions that are getting nowhere, at my desk, in conflicts which can't be resolved, the grey morning brightens and my everyday life takes on another glow. I know that now the risen Christ is with me in the midst of my work. I don't have to struggle to catch something all by myself. The risen Christ gives me hope that life will succeed, even if much seems hopeless. If at his command I cast the net on the right side, on the conscious side, if I work attentively and carefully, the net will be filled. Resurrection takes place in the midst of everyday life, when all at once an impossible knot comes loose, when a conversation gets somewhere, when I can rid myself of my inner tension because I know that now, while I'm sitting at my desk, the risen Christ is with me. I need only be quiet and wait to see what he prompts me to do. Then my life will change. My work will bear fruit.

Where do you encounter the risen Christ? Has he ever come into the night of your frustrations? Where have you experienced a transformation of your everyday life, your grey morning?

Are you familiar with the situation of the disciples on the Emmaus road? What are you running away from? What has disappointed you? What does the risen Christ want to say to you? What could be the meaning of your life? Have you ever found your eyes opened to recognize your real self? Has the mystery of your life ever dawned on you? In that case – Luke thinks – you've seen the risen Christ.

What do you hope for in death? How do you imagine the resurrection that awaits you in death? Can you trust that the love which you now feel will not be destroyed even by death, that as a person you will always be with God, that death will change you into your true form, the glorious form that God intends you to have?

46

Jesus the redeemer

For many Christians the image of the redeemer is probably the image that they associate most closely with Jesus. Jesus has redeemed us. That is the central statement of faith. Redemption means an end to our pains and our distress.

For many Christians redemption above all means liberation from their guilt. For them Jesus is above all the one who frees them from their sins. But the Bible understands redemption in a wider sense. Jesus redeems us by filling our transitory and mortal life with divine life. He redeems us by leading us out of our meaninglessness. Among the many models of redemption that we find in the Bible I shall limit myself to the notion of redemption in Matthew and Luke.

Only in the Gospel of Matthew does Jesus say at the last supper that his blood is 'shed for the forgiveness of sins' (Matthew 26.28). In Matthew Jesus is above all the redeemer from our sins. But how are we to understand the statement that Jesus' blood is shed for the forgiveness of our sins? Isn't that a cruel image of God, if God intends the sacrifice of his son to be able to forgive us? It's certainly not meant in that way. Jesus' blood is an image of his love. Jesus continues to love us up to his death on the cross. Jesus didn't seek death. He proclaimed a merciful God. But at a very early stage he noticed that he was becoming involved in the power play of the politics of his time. The Sadducees felt that he threatened their economic interests. The Romans saw him as a troublemaker. So Jesus became a victim in order that the powerful could hold on to their power. Jesus doesn't react bitterly to the guilty conduct of those who bring him to the cross. He doesn't allow human wickedness to destroy his love. He could have fled. But he stands by his proclamation of the merciful and forgiving God. On the cross he even forgives his murderers.

If I've really burdened myself with guilt, I feel that I can't accept myself. I feel excluded from human company. There are blocks in my unconscious which prevent me from believing in God's forgiveness. But when I look at the cross and see the love of God there, the love that Jesus shows to the end, even to his murderers, these blocks in the unconscious are removed and I can believe not only with my mind but also with my heart that God forgives me, that there is nothing in me that can't be transformed by God's forgiving love.

The cross doesn't bring about the forgiveness of our guilt, but it does make our guilt visible. It communicates God's forgiving love to us. For men and women today, redemption from guilt is a liberating experience. Many people suffer from guilt feelings. They torture themselves with guilt feelings when they feel responsible for the failure of a marriage or the death of a mother. Therapists in their consulting rooms find that the theme of guilt and guilt-feelings crop up in all therapy. Here it's helpful to look at Jesus, who forgives his murderers on the cross. This can help us to give up the mechanism of excusing ourselves and accusing ourselves and to believe in forgiveness.

Luke understands Jesus as redeemer in a different way. The distress from which Jesus frees people is their alienation, their inner dividedness. They've lost themselves. They've missed their way. They've spoilt their lives. In Jesus God visits people in order to bring them back into contact with him and show them the way to a fruitful life. Jesus himself goes ahead of them on their way. In Jesus the image of the true and just person shines out. Luke understands Jesus' life as a drama which culminates in his death on the cross: 'And when all the crowds who had gathered for the spectacle saw what had happened, they went home beating their breasts' (Luke 23.48). God dawns on those who see Jesus hanging on the cross as an image of true humanity. The sight of this divine spectacle transforms them. They beat their breasts. They make contact with themselves. And they go home changed. They've understood the mystery of life and love. For Luke, redemption consists in Jesus sending us his spirit so that we go into the world and shape and form it in that spirit. As Luke sees it, Jesus brought into being a movement that changes the whole world, that increasingly fills it with the healing and liberating love of Jesus and transforms it.

Jesus the redeemer wants to liberate the world with our help from the fetters of unjust rule. He wants to destroy the patterns of life that make people ill, so that they become whole. Through us Jesus wants to open their eyes so that they recognize the meaning of their lives. Freed from meaninglessness, they will discover the way that leads them to true life, by which their lives will bear fruit.

Where do guilt feelings arise in you? How do you deal with your guilt feelings? How do you deal with real guilt? What happens to you when you look at Jesus, who forgives his murderers on the cross? What do you want to be redeemed from? What oppresses you? When do you feel redeemed?

Whether you believe in redemption isn't all that important; the important thing is for Jesus' redeeming activity in the world to become visible through you. Where have you succeeded in loosening fetters, knots, tangles? Where would you like to help today to loosen things up, so that people have more freedom and joy?

47

Jesus – 'I am I'

*The Gospel of John keeps making Jesus say 'Ego eimi' ('I am'). For the Jews
these words were reminiscent of the divine revelation in the burning bush.
There God made himself known under the name 'I am who I am. I am here.'
For me the saying has other associations. Jesus says 'I am I'. Jesus lives out
his selfhood, his unique identity, in a unique way. With this statement he
expresses that he is who he is; he defines himself in terms of himself. He needn't
fulfil the expectations of others, either the pious or the scribes. He is simply
himself. He has the courage to be himself without bothering about what others
think. Jesus is unique. Ultimately he is the end of all questioning. He is simply
'I am I'.*

Luke expresses the same idea in another saying. The risen Jesus says
to his disciples *'Ego eimi autos'* – 'It is myself. I am myself' (Luke 24.39).
The Greek word *autos* to which Luke refers here is an important term
in Stoic philosophy. *Autos* describes the inner sanctuary of the human
being, the true self. It's the inner room of silence into which no noise
penetrates from outside, to which no one has access. It's the room in
which God dwells in human beings. There men and women also come
into contact with the original core of their persons, formed in purity
by God. For Stoic philosophy it was an important task of spiritual
exercises to prevent external things from entering the holy precinct of
the *autos*. If we read the words of Jesus against the background of Stoic
philosophy, he wants us to lead us to our true selves by his resurrection.
The Stoics would say that in his resurrection Jesus makes our selves
impregnable fortresses in which freedom, rest and happiness dwell.

Carl Gustav Jung has developed these notions of Stoic philosophy in our time. He depicts Jesus as the clearest archetype of the self to have appeared in human history. For Jung, Jesus is of course also a historical figure. But because the rabbi from remote Palestine most clearly embodied the archetype of the self, he spoke to the souls of many people, and in a short time conquered the whole world.

By looking at the life of Jesus we can come into contact with the archetypal images which are already lying in our soul. Archetypal images always move something in our soul. They drive us towards our self. Therefore contemplation of the archetypical life of Christ advances the process by which we become human, by which we become ourselves. Jesus is the one who puts us in contact with our self. If we want to go the way of becoming ourselves, it is healthy, indeed necessary, to occupy ourselves with the way of Jesus, from his birth to his death on the cross and his resurrection. Jesus as 'I am I', as the image of the 'self', encourages us to live out our own individuality, to venture on the mystery of our own 'I am I'. Jesus doesn't want to make us dependent on himself but to lead us to our true selves, so that we all live out the unique image that God has made of us.

The early monks understood Jesus as the way to the true human self. They didn't develop any speculative theology, but recommended specific exercises. However, how they ultimately saw Jesus becomes clear in their training programmes. A story is told of a fourth-century monk: Patriarch Poimen said to Patriarch Joseph, 'Tell me how I may become a monk.' He replied, 'If you want to find rest, here and there, then with every action say "I – who am I? And judge no one!"' Becoming a monk means at the same time becoming whole, becoming one with oneself. So it amounts to the question: How does my life bear fruit? How do I achieve harmony with myself?

Try to follow Patriarch Joseph's advice today. Say in all that you do, think and speak, 'I – who am I?' Perhaps this question will lead you to discover your uniqueness. Perhaps through this very question the mystery of Jesus and the mystery of your own person will dawn on you.

Here's another exercise you can try today. Keep repeating to yourself the sentence from the Gospel of Luke, 'I am myself.' Note what this saying does for you. Perhaps you'll discover that masks and roles fall away from you and you penetrate more and more deeply into your true self, your inner sanctuary, in which you are healthy and whole. Then you'll experience Jesus as the one who leads you to your divine and indestructible kernel. When you're in contact with this innermost self you'll have an inkling of what the Gospel of Luke means by resurrection: your self will cross even the threshold of death in safety and shine out clear and pure in God's glory.

48

The Jesus who doesn't let us rest

Every age has tried to understand Jesus in its own way. Every attempt at understanding has plucked new strings in Jesus. But every age has also excluded Jesus from areas that don't fit their notion of him. Every age has commandeered Jesus for its own aims and needs. Jesus will not be forced into an image. He breaks open all images. He will not be taken over. So I ask of all the images that I have described so far: Is that really Jesus? Or am I projecting my own wishes on to him? Who is this Jesus really?

The more I reflect on Jesus, the more I meditate on him, the more images occur to me. I never get to the end of things with Jesus. It's important for me to set Jesus alongside all my experiences, all that I read, see, get to know. What has this Jesus to say to me in the light of my personal situation, in the light of the social and political situation? If I steep myself in other religions and study founders of religions like Buddha, Muhammad or Lao-tse, how do I see Jesus then? What new aspects of Jesus do I discover by practising Zen meditation? What new insights do I have when I study transpersonal psychology? How do I see Jesus when I look at the Jewish tradition and attempt to understand Jesus within Judaism?

One thing always becomes clearer to me when I meditate on Jesus: Jesus isn't a soft cushion on which I can lay my head. I can't misuse Jesus to justify and confirm my way of life. Jesus doesn't confirm, he provokes. He unsettles me. On the one hand he gives me unprecedented freedom. On the other he challenges me. And I can never be content with my life. I can never say like the Pharisees, 'Now I've fulfilled all God's commandments.' Or, 'Now I'm really a disciple of Jesus.' On the one hand Jesus takes away my bad conscience, the feeling that I must always do more. He frees me from the pressure to achieve great things spiritually. On the other hand, he also prevents me from parading my spirituality before others, imagining that through meditation I've already reached my centre, that I'm already completely relaxed and have grown into a deep spiritual experience. Jesus works in a paradoxical way: he gives failures courage to rely on God. He promises them that they're very near to God. But he never allows those who have set out on a spiritual journey to have complete rest. Inexorably he discloses all their shadow sides, their attempts to commandeer God for themselves, to rest on their spiritual laurels, or to feel that they're something special.

Jesus doesn't let me rest. He keeps putting me in question. He remains difficult. I find him uttering marvellous sayings which move me deeply. And I come across sayings which offend me, which I simply can't understand. But it is these provocative sayings of Jesus in particular which prevent me from thinking that I have a complete image of Jesus. Jesus breaks open all my images. He always remains the one who is wholly other. I must keep facing this Jesus anew. Who is he really? What is his real message? What does he want to get me to do today? Here's an example. I take a typical saying of Jesus which doesn't fit our present-day notion of becoming fully human: 'Whoever will be my disciple, let him deny himself, take up his cross and follow me' (Matthew 16.24). Today our concern is to fulfil ourselves, to be true to ourselves. Surely in this saying Jesus didn't mean me to disparage and devalue myself? But 'deny himself' remains a provocation. The Greek word means 'say no, resist'. If I want to be a disciple of Jesus I have to say no to my ego, which retreats hurt and insulted, which puts itself at the centre, makes itself absolute. I must distance myself from the tendency of my ego to claim everything for itself, to make itself the centre of everything. By restraining my superficial wishes and resisting the tyranny of the ego, I can come into contact with my true self. Then I discover who I really am, and what my deepest longing is. And I discover that becoming human also always means bearing the cross. I must accept myself with the conflicting tendencies of my soul, in all my contradictions. That's often painful. But precisely by doing this I discover the life which Jesus calls 'true life'.

Look at the images that you've made for yourself of Jesus. Have you mixed your own projections into these images? Do these images confirm you or do they provoke you?

What sayings of Jesus won't give you rest? What sayings offend you? What challenges you in the difficult sayings of Jesus? What do they want to conjure up in you? What do they want to move you to do?

Sit quietly and listen to yourself: what images of Jesus occur to you? What notions occur to you about who this Jesus really is and what his genuine message is? What does this Jesus want to say to you today?

49

The Jesus who evades us

Many people complain that God is too abstract. So they're helped by imagining Jesus. Jesus makes God concrete to them. That's certainly an important experience that we can have. When I meditate in front of an icon of Christ, God takes on a human face for me. When I imagine that God is looking lovingly at me, I can perceive his love in the eyes of Christ in the icon, which are directed towards me full of loving-kindness. Through Jesus, my relationship with God takes on loving warmth. But at the same time this Jesus keeps disappearing from my sight. I don't have a film of Jesus. I know that the evangelists have always also described Jesus through the spectacles of their own experience. And I know that much of what they say about Jesus is conditioned by their time. Jesus lived in a time that is remote from me.

Who is this Jesus really? Albert Schweitzer said that while the quest of the historical Jesus brought much to light, it failed in its claim to paint a clear picture of Jesus. Jesus keeps disappearing behind the interpretations that people have made of him. There is no consensus over which sayings come from Jesus himself, or over the interpretation that the community gave to the sayings of Jesus.

But precisely because Jesus keeps withdrawing from me, he keeps me alive. Even the images of Jesus that I've described in this book can't give either you or me a clear picture of Jesus. Jesus can shine out for us in these images. But Jesus also keeps withdrawing himself from these images. He's beyond the images. Like God, in the end he can't be captured by an image. The tradition of iconography may believe that with its head of Christ it has made a portrait of the historical Jesus. This tradition begins from the Turin Shroud, which was once in Edessa. The iconographers attempt to get near to this portrait of the face that is depicted on the shroud. But does the Turin Shroud really show us the historical face of Jesus? And even if it depicts the image of Jesus, can I really recognize personal features of Jesus in it? The Old Testament says that we mustn't make any images of God. In the iconoclastic struggle during the seventh century the victory went to those theologians who said that God had become visible to us in Christ and that we might paint this image. But at the same time, here too, we must look through the image and perceive the image behind the images. Jesus can't be captured in any image. The images point to Jesus. But even in them Jesus hides himself.

As a spiritual director I keep meeting people who are looking for a personal relationship with Jesus. They complain that they've neglected their relationship with Jesus or that he has disappeared from their sight. They want to have Jesus as a friend and go through life with him. But even in this image of the friend there is a danger of commandeering Jesus and making for oneself a picture of Jesus which corresponds to one's own longings and not to the historical testimonies to Jesus. Jesus goes with us as the risen Christ. But he also goes with us as he went with the disciples on the Emmaus road. No sooner has he appeared to us than he withdraws from us. And we're alone again. We can't be certain that it's Jesus himself who is accompanying us and leading us into the mystery of life and love; we can't be certain whether we're making for ourselves an image of him which arises out of our own wishes, and if so how.

In our relationship to Christ we must reconcile the tension between experiencing and not experiencing, between image and absence of image, between appearing and becoming invisible. We can't cling on to Jesus. Nevertheless we may trust that the Jesus who lived two thousand years ago, who rose and is sitting at the right hand of the Father, goes with us today, that he is with us and in us. Sometimes I'm certain that now this Jesus is there. Now his word has touched me. Now I feel his presence. Now his face is shining on me. But the very next moment Jesus evades our grasp. We no longer see him, no longer feel his presence. We have the feeling that we have to go on our way alone.

Jesus escapes us when we try to cling on to him. We can only walk in faith and not in sight, in hope and not in certainty.

Try today to offer all that happens to you to this Jesus and to look at it with Jesus. Of course you can't be certain that you're making an image of Jesus. But you'll be certain that you're deliberately looking at yourself. And that's important for your relationship with Jesus. If one pole of the relationship is right, the other pole won't be left completely hanging in the air. If you sense yourself, you may trust that sometimes you'll also sense Jesus.

If you're annoyed at the narrowness of your surroundings then repeat to yourself Jesus' saying, 'Whoever wants to save his life will lose it; but whoever loses his life for my sake will gain it' (Matthew 16.25). Perhaps then, in the specific situation that annoys you, your conflict, your hurt, it will dawn on you who this Jesus could be and what he wants to bring out in you. At the same time you must keep letting go of every image of Jesus that you have and struggle every day to understand this Jesus who accompanies you always and everywhere, but who keeps evading you, so that you go on until you see him for ever.

50

Jesus my life

In his letter to the Philippians Paul writes: 'For me, Christ is life and death is gain' (Philippians 1.21). What experience of Jesus did Paul have, that he could write this sentence?

Exegetes argue about which word is the subject in this sentence. Originally, life was probably the subject. 'For me life is Christ. For me, life consists in Christ.' For Paul, Christ and life are so identical to each other that they're interchangeable. Without Christ his life isn't real life. And he has found all real life in Christ. Without Christ, everything is dead for him; it's only pseudo-life.

Paul experienced personally that Jesus freed him from any pressure to achieve. He no longer needed to earn his own salvation. In Jesus he experienced that someone had died for him and that therefore he was loved unconditionally by God before he had accomplished anything. He no longer had to justify himself and make himself 'righteous'. The love of God which appeared in Jesus had put him right. It had shown him that he might live, that all was well with him, that he had got there. Now he was to live his own life. Christ had freed him to be himself. Now he could breathe again and live. That was the decisive experience in Paul's life. It transformed him utterly from being a narrow-minded and petty man of the law to being a free man who trusted in the grace of God.

In another letter Paul describes his experience like this: 'I have been crucified with Christ: no longer do I live, but Christ lives in me' (Galatians 2.19f.). For Paul the ego, along with the law of this world, has been nailed to the cross with Christ; in other words, all the standards of this world have been 'crossed out', 'abolished'. There is no longer any pressure to achieve, to do everything right. I need no longer go by the expectations of the world or even by the expectations of the spiritual person. I needn't make myself a spiritual person. I needn't make anything of myself. Christ has made something of me. It's no longer my ego that lives, but Christ lives in me. The New Testament scholar Heinrich Schlier put the experience like this. 'The existence of those who have been baptized is no longer grounded in their ego, i.e. in the natural person they have been hitherto, but in the new life that has been created in them ... Christ has entered our being so that we may be translated into the being of Christ.' The experience of Jesus freed Paul from self-centredness, his preoccupation with his human and spiritual maturity and the image he presented to others. In Jesus he experienced the one who raised him to another level, in whom he first experienced what life was.

I'm interested in these words of Paul not for their theological meaning but for the experience that lies behind them. How did Paul experience Jesus? He didn't know him personally at all. He was in the same situation as we are. We haven't seen or heard Jesus. Paul had an inner experience of Jesus. And this inner experience completely changed his life. For Paul, what there had been before this experience was no longer real life. It was only the attempt to fulfil the commandments, to live correctly, to achieve God's grace through his own work. Paul regards his view of life hitherto as nothing but 'rubbish' (Philippians 3.8). Now in this Jesus he's experienced a completely different God, a God who loves him unconditionally. He's also experienced God in a totally new way. Jesus has shown him that he has unassailable worth, that he is loved, with all that he is. And he senses that this Jesus has come so near to him that he actually lives in him. Christ has become his own deepest reality. He no longer acts from the ego but from Christ, who has grown together with him. So he is no longer afraid of persecution or death. For him, all life consists in Christ. And dying is only gain. For in death his longing will be fulfilled and he will be with Christ (Philippians 1.23).

For me, the most urgent question of my life is how I can arrive at Paul's experience of Christ. Sometimes who this Jesus is for me dawns on me in meditation. Then I have an inkling of the truth of Paul's words. But as soon as I want to hang on to this experience, it disappears again. And when I reflect on Paul's words, I no longer know what they really mean. There remains only the intimation that they affect the heart of my struggle, that whether my life bears fruit depends on this experience. When like Paul I experience Christ as my innermost reality, I really live; then I touch on the mystery of life, the mystery of God and my own mystery.

What does your life consist in? All through today try to complete this sentence: 'For me, life is…' Perhaps metaphors will occur to you: 'For me life is like a passing breath, like a blossoming flower, like the rustling of the wind.' If you then keep saying, 'For me life is Christ', what does that mean for you? What kind of taste does this saying leave behind? Is it too abstract, too far removed from your experience? Or do you get some hint of what life really is for you? Do you come into contact with the liberating experience of Jesus: 'You're loved unconditionally, you needn't justify yourself to prove anything. You needn't depict anything. You may simply be, live, feel life.' That's the experience that Jesus gives you: 'You are free to live.'

Part III
Epilogue

How Jesus changes my life

The fifty images of Jesus that I've described have shed a good deal of light on what fascinates me and moves me about Jesus. I've meditated on these images in order to discover more and more about the mystery of Jesus. All of them make me ask how this Jesus, to whom the images point, governs my life. Has my life become different as a result of Jesus.? What specific difference has Jesus made in my life? Would I live differently if I didn't know Jesus? What would change? What have I learned through Jesus? How do I see myself through my encounter with Jesus? How do I see my life? What has Jesus brought about in me? What does Jesus mean for my relationship with God, for my relationship with other people, my daily work, my seeking and struggling for an authentic life? What role does Jesus play in my personal piety? Where in particular do I encounter Jesus? When and where do I have to do with him? How does he shape my thoughts and feelings?

My Jesus prayer

For thirty years I've prayed the Jesus prayer every day. This meditative prayer was practised in early monasticism from the fourth century on and was then widespread above all in the Eastern church. It goes: 'Lord Jesus Christ, Son of God, have mercy on me.' The Eastern church claims that the whole gospel is summed up in this prayer: belief in the incarnation of God in Jesus and in redemption through Christ.

I attune this prayer to my breath. As I breathe in I say silently to myself, 'Lord Jesus Christ', and as I breathe out, 'Son of God, have mercy on me.' I pray this prayer in the morning after choral prayer in my meditation corner, in front of an icon of Christ. I light a candle, sit on a stool and concentrate on my breath. My eyes rest quietly on the icon of Christ. For me this prayer is a good way of allowing myself to be utterly permeated by the spirit of Jesus. I imagine how with my breathing and the words of the prayer Jesus' mercy, Jesus' gentleness and goodness, Jesus' forgiving love and the warmth of his heart are streaming into me and permeating me.

Then if everyday thoughts arise, of conflicts with my brother monks, of problems in administration, of disappointments from people over whom I've taken trouble; if worries, annoyances, sorrow or bitter feelings arise, I deliberately address this prayer to these thoughts and emotions. And sometimes I feel how they change, how Christ becomes an inner reality. The annoyance flies away, the conflict loses power, the bitterness grows less. Then I experience Christ as a sphere in which daily problems are relativized. But I also experience him as a challenge. I can't look at him without holding out to him a heart which often enough has been torn apart. And I can't pray to him and hold on to my resentment at the same time. For me, praying becomes a struggle with Jesus. And it often takes a long time for Jesus to calm the storm of my emotions and illuminate my dark feelings.

Of course sometimes I ask myself whether I'm imagining things. Often enough I sense that I'm getting nowhere with this prayer. Despite intensive practice I remain inwardly empty and distracted. But time and again I may experience that my heart finds rest and that something of the warmth of the merciful love of Jesus streams into my heart. Then Jesus stamps my thoughts and feelings. Jesus directs my action. My thoughts and feelings are no longer governed by my everyday appointments but by Jesus Christ. And I have some idea of Paul's experience. Paul could say: 'I no longer live, but Christ lives in me' (Galatians 2.20). But of course I often find that over the course of the day the effects of this experience disappear. If I'm hurt, sore and bitter feelings overwhelm my heart. It's as if contact with Jesus is broken off. The emotions evoked by the conflicts are more powerful than the reality of Jesus in my heart. Then sometimes I have to keep practising for a long time until Jesus penetrates me so deeply that he cools my heated feelings and brings order into my inner chaos.

Practising the Jesus prayer is like returning to Jesus. Just as the disciples went out in Jesus' name and often enough mixed up Jesus' task with their own purposes and the structures of their own psyche, so too like them I keep returning to Jesus. And I let him tell me: 'Come with me to a solitary place where we are alone, and rest a while' (Mark 6.31). For me, the Jesus prayer is like resting with Jesus. My soul is put in order again. It is once again filled with the Spirit of Jesus. It again becomes transparent to the ground in which Jesus himself dwells in it.

The eucharist as an encounter with Jesus

It's important to me, whenever possible, to celebrate the eucharist every day. In the eucharist I encounter Jesus bodily. There I eat and drink his love incarnate, to be utterly permeated by him. I bring into the eucharist my everyday life, my situation of the moment, my inner mood, and I ask God to transform everything in me and let it be permeated by the Spirit of Jesus.

Two rites above all affect me every day. One rite is the prayer before the transformation, the so-called epiclesis, in which with outstretched hands I call down the Holy Spirit upon the gifts of bread and wine, so that they become the body and blood of Jesus. For me that is the daily prayer that the Holy Spirit will transform my work, my conflicts, my longings and wishes, my disappointments and bitternesses, so that Jesus' spirit shines out in them. I want Jesus to come not only in bread and wine but in all that I think, speak and do. Everything is to make Christ known. And through Christ everything is to become bread and wine for men and women, something that feeds them and gladdens their hearts.

The second rite is communion. In eating the bread and drinking the wine I take Jesus into myself bodily. In the wine, Jesus' love streams into me and gives me a new taste. All through my body I feel that I'm permeated by Jesus' love. I try to rely on Jesus with all my senses and with the deepest longing of my heart. I hope that the taste of Jesus' love doesn't just remain a momentary feeling but transforms my relations with my fellow men and women and my work. I think about specific features of my work, about meeting difficult brother monks, about my fellow workers and the people to whom I give advice. If I meet people in the awareness that Jesus is in me and also in them, how would I look at them and address them? This notion frees me from the burden that sometimes lies on me when I think of the many people who want something of me today and who overload me with their problems.

Jesus and my relationship to God

Through Jesus God takes on a human face for me. Precisely when I have no sense of God, when God hides himself behind the many concepts and images which I have of him, looking at Jesus helps me. I see the man Jesus, how he speaks, how he deals with others, how he looks them lovingly in the eye and touches them, and think to myself, 'God shines out in this man.' When I look at Jesus, I can't make any image of God for myself. God becomes clear in Jesus as someone who believes in men and women, who accepts them unconditionally, who opens their eyes to recognize true reality.

When I'm quiet in order to pray, doubts often arise in me. Is God merely a figment of my imagination, a creation of mine to help me live more easily? Who is God really? Is God just a personal power who permeates everything? When such questions and doubts come over me, it helps me to look at Jesus. Jesus existed. In him I'm confronted with God. When I meditate on images of Jesus I can't avoid God. For this Jesus speaks of God. In Jesus God becomes concrete. In him God turns to me as the one who forgives, the one who encourages, the one who has mercy. He shines out for me as the one who addresses me, looks at me, touches me, encounters me. Then what Jesus promised Philip dawns on me: 'Whoever has seen me has seen the Father' (John 14.9). I meditate on these word and ask myself: If that's the case, how then do I experience myself, my fellow human beings, creation?

In this Jesus the mystery of God and the mystery of life dawn on me. When I look on Jesus, my relationship with God becomes warmer and more human.

Jesus and my relationship to my neighbour

Jesus keeps drawing the disciples' attention to their neighbours. They encounter Jesus himself in their fellow men and women. Jesus probably expressed this most urgently in his words at the last judgement: 'I was hungry and you gave me food, I was thirsty and you gave me drink, I was a stranger and homeless and you welcomed me; I was naked and you clothed me; I was sick and you visited me; I was in prison and you came to me' (Matthew 25.35f.).

We are to see Christ in all our fellow human beings. But how can we do that? After all, we can't see this specific Jesus in everyone. I find it helpful to imagine that everyone is a brother or a sister of Jesus. There's a divine kernel in all of us. In everyone there is the self, and Christ dwells in this self. This self is ultimately Christ. Christ is the innermost kernel of every human being. In all human beings there is a mystery which transcends them. Every human being is affected by the incarnation of God in Jesus Christ. God's face shines out in every human being.

But to see Christ in others is more for me than a theological explanation of the indwelling of Christ in every human being. In concrete terms it means that I may not fixate myself on the outward appearance of my fellow human beings. I must look through this outward appearance to their innermost being. And there is a kernel of good in everyone. For in everyone there is the face of Jesus Christ. The attempt to see Christ in others isn't primarily a moral demand on me, but a demand of faith. Faith means not only believing in God but also believing in our fellow human beings, having confidence that there is a kernel of good in each of them. Pessimism, mistrust and contempt of others are signs of a lack of faith in God. My relationship with others raises the question of God, i.e. the question of where God is visible. Jesus has taught me that God is to be found in human beings and that any love of God becomes a farce if it doesn't show itself in the concrete love of others. With this message Jesus never lets me rest. Time and again he comes to me with another face.

Belief that Christ is in every human being has political consequences. Jesus calls on us to see him particularly in those who live on the margins, who are hungry and thirsty, who are prisoners and naked. Jesus prevents me from settling down comfortably in my spirituality. He directs my gaze away from myself to those on the periphery, to the unjust structures which drive people into poverty. If I believe that Christ is in every human being, I can't distinguish between desirable and undesirable persons; I must be ready to accept everyone – foreigners, asylum-seekers and all those people who do not correspond to my view of what it is to be human.

Jesus and my experience with
other religions

When at the end of the 1960s I couldn't cope with many forms of our monastic spirituality, I practised Zen meditation with my fellow monks and studied Buddhism and Hinduism. The spiritual experience of both religions fascinated me. Dialogue with other religions has changed my view of Jesus.

Buddhism has opened my eyes to Christian mysticism, which is already present in the Gospel of John and the letters of Paul. In dialogue with Buddhism I came to understand in a new way some of the words used by Jesus, like 'repent', *metanoeite*. This word used to have a moralizing and pessimistic tone for me. As a result of my encounter with Buddhism it has dawned on me that Jesus invites us to look behind things, to perceive the real behind the appearances, to recognize the divine world behind the world of seeming. Hinduism has taught me to look more closely at the tension between multiplicity and unity which Jesus represents in his person and which he himself talks about in the farewell discourses in the Gospel of John. Jesus makes it possible for me to experience oneness in my dividedness, oneness with myself, with others, with creation and with God, the ground of all being.

The New Testament authors were already engaged in dialogue with other religions. Luke sketched out his portrait of Jesus against the background of Greek philosophy and mythology. 2 Peter draws a portrait of Jesus in dialogue with Hellenistic syncretism. This syncretism was a combination of the religions of Persia, Egypt and Greece. The authors of the New Testament took up concepts and notions from the world of other religions and used them to interpret Jesus. So it's legitimate to discover new aspects of Jesus by looking at other cultures and religions.

When I was in Korea in May 2001 it became clear to me how important it is to look at Jesus with new eyes in dialogue with Confucianism and Buddhism. There Jesus encounters me above all as a teacher and a spiritual master. Jesus proclaimed in simple words a spiritual way which is quite the equal to that of Buddha.

I'm not concerned to see Jesus as the founder of one religion among others. For me he is and remains the son of God. In him God has revealed himself in a unique way. For me he is – as Karl Rahner has put it – God's absolute communication of himself. But we Christians are far from having exhausted the mystery of Jesus. We keep looking at him only from the perspective of our Western culture and are blind to certain areas that he also embodies.

Dialogue with other religions may open our eyes to recognize in Jesus the divine riches which have become visible in him. If I honestly engage in dialogue with other cultures, a new love of Jesus grows in me. In them I sense what I have in Jesus. But at the same time it also offends me that we Christians have often obscured this Jesus, that we've used him to set ourselves above others, that we've misused him as a weapon to fight all those with other beliefs.

What fascinates me about Jesus

Finally I would like to make a personal confession about what fascinates me about Jesus. Here I note a development in my picture of Jesus and my relationship to Jesus.

In my youth Jesus was above all a model for me. This model inspired me. It drove me to work on myself so that I could come to resemble it. As a boy I fought against my errors and weaknesses in order to follow Jesus. For me he was above all the image of the good and helpful, free and authentic human being.

Then at the end of my studies I became familiar with the Jesus of mysticism. Above all I read the words of Jesus in the Gospel of John. What fascinated me about this mystical Jesus was the idea that Jesus dwells in me, that through him I discover my original and authentic being and he becomes my true self, that Jesus fills me with divine life and leads me to unity with God.

In recent years my relationship to Jesus has changed again. Now my main concern is how Jesus shapes my everyday life and how by shaping and enduring the conflicts of everyday life I increasingly grow into the figure of Jesus. Whether or not I believe in Jesus isn't primarily a matter of believing in the right creed, in repeating theological formulae. For me, whether or not I believe in Jesus becomes evident from whether in everyday conflicts and disappointments, in experiences of being misunderstood and feeling lonely, of being hurt and forsaken, I become bitter and hard, or whether I allow myself to be shaped by the spirit of Jesus. Whether or not I believe in Jesus becomes particularly evident when no one supports me, and others insult me and rub salt in old wounds. Jesus didn't become hard in such situations. He faced even hostility from his inner source of love. Even on the cross he continued to love. For me that's a challenge to allow myself to be filled with the spirit of Jesus in the conflicts and controversies of my everyday life. I know the temptation to be bitter, to become hard, in order to be unassailable. But precisely when I sense bitter and hate-filled feelings in myself, it's important for me to offer them to Jesus. Such situations decide whether or not I'm a disciple of Jesus, whether I'm wholly caught up with my bitterness or whether I make room in myself for the gentleness and mercy of Jesus. Then each everyday situation becomes a challenge to take Jesus seriously in my life and to follow him.

Jesus protects me on my spiritual way from the illusion that I've already become completely relaxed and spiritual. In the midst of the emotions which arise in me and seek to dominate me, Jesus rises up in me to invite me to 'deny myself', to say no to the demands of my ego and thus grow into a greater freedom. Jesus is the key to my life. He keeps opening the door that I must go through in order really to breathe in his spirit and allow myself to be filled with his love. And I sense how every day the important question for me is whether I shut myself off inwardly or whether I allow myself to be opened up by Jesus to love, mercy and gentleness. That's what being a disciple of Jesus means for me.

I know the great sayings about the one who follows Christ, leaves self aside and simply serves others unselfishly. The older I get, the more critical of such great sayings I become. I know what an everyday matter spirituality is. Every conflict, every criticism, every disappointment, every hurt, decides on whether I'm following my hurt ego or Jesus, who leads me into another dimension, the dimension of God. Here the Gospel of Luke has become important for me. By meditating on the life of Jesus Luke came to understand that 'we must attain the kingdom of God through many tribulations' (Acts 14.22). The Greek word *thlipsis* means oppression, trouble, friction, hurt. My way to the kingdom of God or the *doxa theou*, the glory of God, the unique and glorious form which God has made of me, leads through many oppressions, inside and out, through what the mystic Johannes Tauler calls the 'throng'. On this way, many external shells which distort this primal image of God in me will be peeled off. Through the everyday throng Jesus' form will shine out ever more clearly in me.

To sum up my confession of Jesus, I would want to say that for me Jesus is the one who gives God a human face. When God disappears in my theorizing, he shines out again for me in the figure of Jesus as a human God, as a God who encounters me as one to whom I can speak, as a God who raises me up, frees me, redeems me, forgives me, gives me breadth, freedom and love. Jesus is the one who frees me from the pressure to achieve great things spiritually. On his cross, Jesus 'crossed out' all human ideas of a spiritual way. On the cross he also 'crossed out' all my ideas of God and myself, in order to open me up to the mystery of life.

For me, Jesus is the message that I am accepted unconditionally by God. And for me Jesus is the guarantee that love drives out all fear. Jesus has lived out God's love for me so convincingly that I may cast aside all fear of incurring guilt, of failure and damnation. For me Jesus is the visible manifestation of the message that 'God is love and whoever abides in love abides in God and God abides in him. There is no fear in love, but perfect love casts out fear' (1 John 3.16,18). For me Jesus is the love of God incarnate. When it permeates me I am whole, redeemed and free. That is the hope that inspires me. That is the foundation on which I believe. That is the love by which I live.